TRUCKER GHOST

And Other True Tales of Haunted Highways, Weird Encounters, and Legends of the Road

Within the pages of this book are the real-life accounts of people who have done or seen things on the road that they would never have believed . . . if they hadn't personally lived through them.

Here are just a few:

In "UFO Encounter in Wyoming," a peaceful journey under the open night sky, guided by the Northern Lights, is shattered by an explosive alien encounter.

The teens of "The Cross on the Car" go for a joyride through a cemetery and discover that sometimes the dead are not truly gone . . .

A familiar drive home in Pittsburgh takes a turn into the "Turnpike to the Twilight Zone" when the driver detours into a parallel universe.

Halloween at midnight on "The Bloody Bride Bridge" proves to a college freshman the doomed specter of local legend is actually a chilling reality.

A young, dark-haired girl in a truck is an "Uninvited Passenger" who fades right into thin air.

So, buckle up and get ready for a road trip of trucker ghost stories told by people driving through the uncanny mysteries of night and fog of America's haunted highways and byways . . .

Books by Annie Wilder

Trucker Ghost Stories (anthology)*
Spirits Out of Time
House of Spirits and Whispers

*A Tor Book

TRUCKER GHOST STORIES

And Other True Tales of Haunted Highways,

Weird Encounters, and Legends of the Road

EDITED BY ANNIE WILDER

TOR®

A Tom Doherty Associates Book

New York

A Tor Book
Published by Tom Doherty Associates, LLC
175 Fifth Avenue
New York, NY 10010

www.tor-forge.com

Tor® is a registered trademark of Tom Doherty Associates, LLC.

ISBN 978-0-7653-3035-2 (trade paperback)
ISBN 978-0-4299-2458-0 (e-book)

First Edition: August 2012

Printed in the United States of America

0 9 8 7 6 5 4 3

Dedicated to the memory of Bill Sykes

—A.W.

Acknowledgments

I would like to thank the following people for their help in making this book happen.

Terry L. Aldershof contributed two great stories, and his foreword captures exactly the "late nights on deserted roads" feeling that is the book's theme. He was there to fill whatever role I needed while putting this book together: a sounding board, a source of support, and someone who could credibly answer questions about truckers and their experiences.

Early on in this project, Samuel Barradas and volunteers Paul Brickman and Duckslayer at TruckersReport helped get out the word about this book project. Thanks to them, and to everyone at TruckersReport who lent a hand in this endeavor.

A lot of people in both the paranormal and trucker worlds, in radio and on the Web, also helped spread the word. My sincere thanks and a shout-out to the following friends, old and new:

Dave Schrader and Mallie Fox of DarknessRadio.com; Jim Harold, host of the Paranormal Podcast and author of *Jim Harold's Campfire;* Marco Beghetto of *Today's Trucking;* Stan Campbell of *The Driver Show;* Jerry Puffer of KSEN in Montana; Woody Nelson of *Cowboy Bill's Radio;* Hervy at *Life as a Trucker;* and Trucker Fred.

A number of the stories came from popular paranormal and ghost story Web sites. Such sites contain a wealth of true experiences of ghostly encounters, and I couldn't have produced this book without the cooperation and assistance of the people who created and manage the following Web sites:

Stephen Wagner of Paranormal.About.com, Don Wilmshurst of CastleofSpirits.com, Martin of YourGhostStories.com, Kathy Weiser of LegendsofAmerica.com, and Justin Jimenez of Exam iner.com.

A big thanks to family friend Sarah Cothran for recommending HARO (HelpaReporter.com) as a possible source for storytellers. And thanks to HARO.

Thanks, too, to the many friends and acquaintances who helped spread the word and scout out stories for the book—especially Christy Devillier, Jennifer Spees, Jody Lowder, and Amy Pittack.

Thanks also are due to David Schulte, who was an invaluable help with transcribing stories and providing clear and concise tech advice when needed (which was often) . . . and a source of fresh mint tea!

My agent, Weronika Janczuk, and Bob Diforio of the D4EO agency have rocked in every way at every step of this process. Ditto for Jim Frenkel, my editor at Tor Books. Huge thanks to all of them for their knowledge and expertise, and for being fun to work with, to boot. And thanks to Angela Gibson, for the excellent copyediting.

A heartfelt thanks to my mate, Dudley Parkinson, for being strong and steady and supportive—helping with everything from pursuing story leads to printing permissions forms to making dinner so I could keep working.

Finally, and most important, I would like to express my sincere thanks to each person who contributed a story.

Contents

PART 2
MESSAGES AND ASSISTANCE FROM THE SPIRIT WORLD

PART 3
HAUNTED HIGHWAYS: LEGENDS AND LORE OF THE ROAD

PART 4
TIME SLIPS

Foreword

I was asked once what makes a real truck driver. It takes a very special type of person to drive truck for a living; we are nomadic, like Gypsies. Our home is where our truck is. We were here long before the interstate highway system was created. We have names like Gandalf, Iron Horse, Freeway, and Patches. We speak a language unique unto ourselves, and, like the ancient mariners, we gather to share our stories.

It is easy enough to recognize the "real truck driver." We are the person sitting alone at the counter drinking coffee while everyone else is asleep in their beds. We are the lone set of headlights on the dark, winding, two-lane road, hauling a load that no one else would touch, under conditions that would keep any sane driver safe at home. We are the one driver willing to go to some faceless little town in the middle of nowhere—somewhere the average driver will never see or even know the name of.

We chase the Northern Lights as they flicker and dance across northern Minnesota and the plains of North Dakota; we chase them unhampered into the wild expanses of Montana and Wyoming. As we pass alone in the middle of the night through places like Wounded Knee and Little Big Horn, we have seen the ghost riders and heard the screams of anguish from the spirits of the dead.

We run the back roads through the swamps and bayous of Louisiana and Mississippi. We travel on deserted roads, where the glow of the full moon is dappled by Spanish moss that hangs heavy across the roadway from the branches of ancient sycamores. We have seen the bonfires that light up the night, and we have heard the chants and wailing songs from the undead. We have been to places with names like Old Salem and Jamestown, settlements that were founded 146 years or more before the signing of the Declaration of Independence, settlements that burned witches at the stake. Alone, in the darkest hours before dawn, as our headlights cut a path through the dense forest, we are the ones that are flagged down by these gossamer-clad apparitions.

As we sit in a nearly empty diner perched on the edge of nowhere, we take a few minutes to talk to a lonely soldier and reminisce about a war that once raged a half a world away. We will remember that soldier's name—for had it not been for him and the time we shared, we would have been part of the fatal accident that occurred sixty miles up the road. It will come as no surprise to us when, some twenty-five years later, we find that same soldier's name inscribed on a black granite wall in Washington, D.C. We say a silent prayer. For, unlike us, he never made it home.

These are our stories—stories told by real truck drivers and by their families and colleagues in the transportation world. Many of these stories have been handed down from father to son, and then on again to our sons and daughters. They are our stories; we know and understand the tales of the road.

If you meet us, you will be able to recognize us by what they call the thousand-yard stare in our eyes—for we have seen so much more than you ever will.

I have driven professionally for over thirty-three years, and have traveled nearly six million miles behind the wheel of a semi-truck. I've hauled everything from artichokes to elephants, in and through the contiguous forty-eight states, three provinces of Canada, and farther north, including the Yukon and Alaska. I am a real truck driver; the stories my colleagues and I share with you here are our stories—for we have lived them.

—Terry L. Aldershof

Introduction

This is a collection of true ghost stories, unexplained or paranormal encounters, and legends and lore of the road. A majority of the stories are from truckers or others associated with truckers and the transportation industry: diesel mechanics, trucking company security guards, truckers' ex-wives or ex-girlfriends. Other stories came from people who are not truckers but whose stories made the cut because they're great stories that reveal the very scary, strange things that can occur on seemingly ordinary nights while driving deserted highways, back roads, and byways—and, maybe, somewhere near you.

These firsthand accounts are as varied as the storytellers themselves—some are detailed and filled with emotion, others are brief and straightforward retellings of truly chilling events. Most take place in the United States, but some of the stories come from far away—as far as Australia and Slovakia.

There's a story of a ghost rider on old Highway 666 in New Mexico, a phantom truck (not 309) that saved a driver's life, ghost trains and soldiers, UFOs, a prom girl ghost in Alabama, a demon in Texas, and a shadow person in Charlotte, among other tales. My own haunted highway experience, which was so bizarre that for years I didn't talk about it (except with my sister, who was with me when it happened), appears in the "Messages and Assistance from the Spirit World" section.

I got the idea for this book because I love true ghost stories—hearing or reading them as well as telling them—and because when I was thirteen years old, a truck driver named Bill Sykes told me a ghost story. It was 1975, and I had a summer job answering the phone and typing invoices at the sand-mining plant my dad managed in Woodbury, Minnesota. The truckers would come into the office while they waited for their trucks to be loaded with silica sand or flour. Sykes, a rail-thin fellow who wore cowboy boots and a big chain on his wallet, was mostly silent around my dad and other men, but if there was no one else around, he'd tell me interesting stories from his life or that he'd heard while driving.

I don't remember all the details of Bill's ghost story, I'm sorry to say—it was something about a little ghost girl, and Bill knew someone who, encountering the ghost girl, put his fingers on her wrist to see if she had a pulse (she didn't, of course). But I can still clearly picture Bill as he told me the story—a solemn expression on his deeply lined face, his gleaming black hair (always slicked back with hair cream) falling forward as he tipped his head down and peered at me over his glasses. I thought the story was scary and cool, and I wanted Bill to tell it to my dad and the other guys at the sand plant, but he wouldn't—he said a lot of people didn't believe in ghosts and he only told ghost stories to people who appreciated them. Now, decades later, I wonder if Bill ever told this story to anyone else or if it's been lost forever.

I have thoroughly enjoyed reading these ghost stories as they came in, browsing through posts on online forums about truckers' weird experiences, and talking to people on the phone as they shared their haunted road stories. I think that Bill, who passed away some years ago, would have enjoyed these stories, too.

—Annie Wilder

PART I

Just Plain Weird

A seemingly ordinary road leads an unsuspecting driver into another dimension. A trucker grabbing a few hours of sleep at a rest stop gets a lingering kiss from someone who isn't there. A businessman on a road trip undergoes a life-changing contact experience with extraterrestrial beings at a truck stop.

These stories will challenge your understanding of the very nature of reality. Most of these folks did not believe in ghosts, UFOs, aliens, or Bigfoot and other creatures of his ilk—until they actually encountered them face-to-face. These just plain weird collisions with the inhabitants of otherworldly realms sometimes take place on lonely roads in the dead of night, sometimes on busy highways in the bright light of day, even, on a few terrifying occasions, right beside the driver *inside* the vehicle.

DEMON IN TEXAS

Well, I was in this place in Texas, off of this road that was said to be an Indian burial ground. They had mulch after the hurricane, Hurricane Ike. They had mulch and stuff on that piece of land, on that property—lots of it. This subcontractor called me to have it hauled away. So I called up a couple guys I'd been working with, and we ran that site for a good two weeks. And as I was completing the job, I stayed on-site because we didn't have anywhere else to go and we didn't have a job; we weren't welcome on the work site, so me and a friend of mine stayed on that property. And then at night we would sleep in our trucks. So this one night we were sleeping there and it was very, very cold. A little snow was on the ground.

So I remember about like 8:00 P.M., we went to bed early. I was laying down with my head somewhat by the window. I had a 1995 Freightliner SLD—it's a flattop, and there's a single bed. So I was on the bed, lying down. And I heard a commotion outside the truck. I'm saying to myself, "What's all the commotion?!" The wind was just howling and going on like crazy. I felt my truck shaking like it wanted to turn over. It was like the wind was blowing something like sixty miles an hour. All of a sudden the wind just picked up and just started acting *crazy*.

Anyway, I hear the commotion again outside, like folks talking. And I'm wondering to myself, "Who on earth is over here making noise at my head?" I'm thinking out loud, and I'm saying, "It's just me and my buddy over here, in the truck." And I'm hearing the noise of talking; and the wind's blowing hard . . . while I'm saying, "Man, this is just crazy."

I felt like a hand came through the side window, which is the window to the back of the truck, the little breathing window. I felt a hand touching me on the head. I start throwing my elbow and trying to hit the hand. I'm trying to shove the hand from off of my head. And the touch went away. Then I heard the wind pick up some more, and then I heard somebody trying my door! My door was locked. So when I heard the person trying my door, I didn't say anything 'cause the truck was fully locked. I didn't worry about anyone coming in on me. I had the windows wound up and the door locked. I had a plastic bag on my brake lever. And I heard, like, the wind coming *inside* of my truck now. I mean, I hear the wind just howling inside the truck. And it was just making a *lot* of horrible noise, picking up the plastic bags and tearing at everything I have. And I'm saying, "Lord? What is this going on?" You know what I'm saying?

My back was turned to the steering end of the truck, the front of the truck. I had my back turned. I was lying in the back of the truck. And I felt a pressure come and lay on top of me, trying to pin me down on the bed. I'm crying out for the Lord, and I'm saying, "Lord, Jesus Christ of Nazareth, have mercy. The blood of

Jesus is upon you." I'm crying out and I'm saying it *real loud*. I could hardly hear myself talking, 'cause it felt like my tongue was so heavy that I couldn't get a word out. But I was *still* saying it in my mind. And I'm trying to speak and I couldn't speak. But I'm saying it in my mind—I'm saying, "The blood of Jesus is against you." Until I felt it lift off of me. All I saw was my curtains thrown back, and I heard it go through the door . . . *thwip!* As if a knife was chopping something. It went straight through my door.

I turned my lights on . . . and I got the Bible, and I started to read and pray to the Lord. My friend, who was next door to me in his truck, heard nothing. And he said he got up and saw my lights turned on and asked himself what I was doing up at three o'clock in the morning. He didn't hear me screaming. He didn't hear *anything*.

There's a house down here in Missouri City, Texas. A friend of mine owns it. So he asked us to stay there. I parked my truck outside, and I slept in my truck when I came down Friday and I stayed from Friday till today. I didn't go in the house and sleep, because that house is terrible! But I slept in my truck. I heard demons coming to my truck. But they couldn't come in. I specifically bought *The Passion of the Christ* tape, and I played it in my truck *loud*. And when it cut off, I heard the demonic forces coming toward the truck and pulling on my door. It was the same wind blowing—it happened this weekend. And I felt the presence come into the truck. But it couldn't come into the cab where I was. And I just got up, turned on the DVD, let it play. And it was peaceful again, and I went back to sleep.

—George Stern, Sr.

CHASED BY A LIGHT

I was leaving Hobart, Tasmania, on a summer night in 2002. It was about 2:00 to 3:00 A.M., and I was heading to Launceston, which is a drive of about two and a half hours, 240 kilometers (about 150 miles) on the open highway. Being that time of the morning, the road was dead quiet. There were no cars about—I was so bored by the trip, I actually counted cars going either way. I only passed one car going to Launceston and three heading the other way in the whole trip.

I was familiar with the road, as I had traveled it for work many times before and have many times since (but only one of those times since what happened has been at night—and I wasn't alone). The highway has a history of accidents, including many fatalities, as you would expect with any main highway.

It was a clear night, and I was about thirty minutes into my trip, and in a hurry to get home. Now what you have to keep in mind is that the whole trip is through rural areas. Sure, there are a couple of little towns along the way, but they are small towns that usually closed by 8:00 P.M. and there are no streetlights or anything, so when you're out driving at these times, you can usually see any vehicles' lights a mile away.

I was driving along, listening to my music, when I noticed a red light some distance behind me in my rearview mirror. At first I thought to myself, "That's strange; I didn't pass any cars." I just put it down to another car's taillights and thought nothing else of it.

After another few minutes, I checked my mirror only to find the lights were still there, some two hundred yards behind me. At this point, I started to slow down to see what it was, but the red light stayed the same distance behind me, so I increased my speed, but, again, the light stayed the same distance behind. I started to think it must be some crazy reflection of my taillights, so I actually turned my lights off, but the light was still there!

No matter what I did, this strange red light followed. The only time it would disappear was when I would go around a corner—it would disappear, only to come around the corner when I was about two hundred yards farther down the road. This cat-and-mouse game continued for about fifteen to twenty minutes, with me watching it as much as I could while driving; then I went around a corner and it never came around, so it was over.

Or so I thought.

About ten minutes or so after the red light had stopped following me I noticed a white light in a field about two hundred yards off the road to my right. Now, since it was a farming area, my first thought was, "Oh, it's someone out hunting by spot-light," which is quite a common thing in these areas. But then, as my car passed the area where the light was I noticed it started to keep pace with my car.

Now by this time, I'm starting to freak out a little and start-ing to look for a reasonable explanation for the light and how it could keep up with my car. I wound down my window to see if it was a reflection on the glass, but no, it was still there.

I turned off my lights. Again, no difference.

I slowed down, sped up, but it stayed right beside me, never getting closer or moving away. It was at this time that I noticed something that for some reason really freaked me out—the white light was jumping the boundary fences! Every time it got to the end of the field, it would rise up four feet, go over the fences, and drop back down again. This little fact set me into a panic, since if it was a trick of light reflection, why would it jump the fences? The sickening thought sunk in that this was real, and by now I had started to panic. I thought whatever this was wanted me for some reason.

My instincts told me, just get to the next town, and you will be okay. So I went as fast as my car would go, and either a police-man would pull up (and hopefully prove I wasn't losing my mind) or I would reach the next town. Either way, I would lose this "follower."

The light continued to follow me for what seemed like an eternity, until about a thousand yards out of the town, then it just vanished. It never appeared again for the rest of my trip . . . thankfully.

The strange thing is, I am no newcomer to strange things happening. I lived in two haunted houses prior to this event and had some freaky situations in them, but something about this just spooked me. Even to this day, it sends chills up my spine—maybe because whatever this was, it was toying with me, and no matter what I did to get away, I couldn't.

—Scott Wood

THE GIRL IN THE WINDOW

Hey, my name is Matt McFadden; this is my story that happened while I was trucking for a combine harvest crew. It happened in northern Saskatchewan; it was around 10:00 P.M. or so. I had just gotten a load of wheat and I was heavy, but it had been like that all day. At night I mostly run in the center or on the centerline of the road. (The lights on my rig don't go that far out and aren't real bright.)

So I'm going down the road. It's dark, no moon, there's no houses on this road, so I figure I won't see anyone because I hadn't yet passed anyone on the road. But for some reason, I decided to hold my lane. I'm moving right along, and I happened to look out my window on the driver's side for some reason. I saw a face looking up at me. It was a girl in her late teens or early twenties, with dark hair, but that's all I could really see. She was on the centerline. I couldn't tell you if she was floating, tall, or an optical illusion, just that her face was there, clear as day. Which is odd, because I was watching the road and the ditches for deer. But there was a face, looking me right in the eye.

I looked in my mirror; then, I radioed to ask the next trucker if he saw anything—we both saw nothing. I asked the farmer the next day if anyone lived in the area, he said no one, nothing has ever lived where I saw her. But she was there.

—Matt McFadden

UFO ENCOUNTER IN WYOMING / U.S. HIGHWAY 26

In the mid-1970s, I was leased to a trucking company called International Transport out of Rochester, Minnesota. We had at the time a satellite terminal in Kalispell, Montana, where we would load lumber out of if we were in that area. There were three trucks in the area when this happened. We spent the day loading and tarping our loads and headed for a small town outside of Indianapolis that evening. We all spent the night just north of Yellowstone National Park and headed out in the morning. It was early winter, and the roads were virtually empty. We decided to angle across east out of Idaho Falls to save time and miles. In Wyoming, we picked up U.S. Highway 26, which we would follow to Casper.

We pulled into Shoshoni around 8:00 P.M. that night. We ate and fueled, then headed east. It was a beautiful night, and the Northern Lights were out, dancing across the northern sky. This was during the time that there were reported cattle mutilations across the Dakotas, so that was one of the topics of conversation that night.

Once you leave Shoshoni, it is almost three hundred miles to Casper, the most beautiful but desolate road you will ever see in your life. CB radios were just coming into vogue, and it was a real treat if you had someone you could run with that had one, too. The three of us had radios, and we decided to stay together so we would have someone to talk to. We stayed about two miles apart and spent the evening talking about one thing or another, mainly just pissing and moaning about the company and the loads.

There was what looked to be a meteor shower that night; the sky was alive with lights and burning trails. With no city lights to obstruct the view, it was absolutely breathtaking. It was about two o'clock in the morning when the lead truck came on the radio telling whoever was behind him to quit screwing around and get rid of the high beams. Then a few minutes later, he was asking where we disappeared to. A few minutes after that, he would say that he saw us again. It was a little confusing as we were at least two miles apart. I was in the middle, and I knew for a fact that I didn't see his trailer lights. The more he talked about the bright lights in his mirror, the more meteors there were in the sky.

We started joking that he needed to keep his eyes on the road and not the night sky. He started getting really agitated, swearing at us, calling us names; then he apparently sped up to get away from us because his signal was getting weaker. I asked him where he was going in such a hurry, and he told me he just wanted me off of his ass.

His radio was getting scratchy and began to break up, like he was pulling away from us and almost out of range. I sped up in order to keep him in radio range, and told the truck behind me to do the same. We were flying along this empty road when we came to a set of hills. The third hill we came to had a really bright light just on the other side, but as we crested the top of the hill, the light went out. Before I realized it, I was less than a hundred feet away from the back end of the truck in front of me. He was stopped right in the middle of the road with no lights on. I slammed on my brakes and told the truck behind me to do the same or he would hit me, too. I slid right past the stopped truck before I finally got stopped myself. The last truck pulled to the shoulder behind the truck in the middle of the road. As I got out of the truck, I could smell burning rubber and wood; it was hanging heavy in the cold night air. When I got beside the truck, the driver of the last truck was already standing there with his mouth hanging open, staring at the driver inside the cab. The truck was sitting lopsided; every tire on that side was flat and still smoldering. His windshield was burned black and had exploded, as did the driver's door glass. His truck was dark green and school-bus yellow as were ours (company colors), but it was black now, at least one side of it was. The paint was blistered and peeling off of the door and sleeper. His tarps had melted to the wood underneath, which was burnt completely through and was still smoldering and smoking like it had been used as a giant bonfire, then put back.

We opened the driver's door to find the driver sitting there staring out the windshield like he was dead; his left sleeve was burnt crisp and stuck to his arm, which was also burned almost black. His face was burnt on the left side, and his hair was completely gone. He was bleeding out of the cracks in his skin, and he was having trouble breathing. We spent about an hour getting him out of his truck and into mine and his truck out of the middle of the road. The trip to the hospital was nearly two hours, and he spent the whole trip talking about the bright lights, asking me if I had seen them. I told him I hadn't, just the lights in the sky. He grabbed my arm at one point and started screaming that they tried to get him out of his truck—but he wouldn't let them take him. The lights had forced him to stop his truck, and then in a matter of seconds they were trying to pry open his door. He said he locked it and pulled as hard as he could to keep it shut, but it kept opening in spite of his efforts. There were dozens of tiny lights hovering and maneuvering around his truck, four or five larger stationary lights, and at the end there was one huge blinding light, which must have been the light I saw over the horizon. He said there were half a dozen of these things walking around his truck touching it, shaking it, and trying to get inside. They were tall, tall enough to look inside the window of a cab-over truck while still standing on the ground. I only come to just below the middle of the door, and I am 6'2".

At the hospital, they sedated him when they admitted him. I didn't see him again for almost three months, but they towed his truck into Rochester, where it sat in the corner of the yard for almost two years. He suffered second- and third-degree burns over 25 percent of the left side of his body and lost the sight in his left eye. I personally have never seen a UFO, but to this day, I will swear that my friend has.

—Terry L. Aldershof

SHADOW PERSON IN CHARLOTTE

Driving on the road with a big truck, you see all kinds of people. One day, I was delivering a load in Charlotte, North Carolina. It was at about eleven in the morning, in the springtime. The day was sunny and clear. I had to get on the interstate to go one exit over for the delivery. I was on I–77 near the I–85 split in Charlotte. Near the end of the entrance ramp to I–85 was what looked like a homeless person. He had his bags by his side, and there were a few trees and bushes in the area to obscure the bright sunlight of the day. As I passed him, I saw this figure was a man, but he was matte black. There were no skin-toned features visible on him, and no shiny spots that suggested he was sweating. He had long black hair, and his clothes were crumpled in outline, but even that was matte black. I noticed him, and saw through my side mirrors that he ducked back under the bushes. I got a chill after I saw him. It has been said that there are shadow people that appear in this world, and I think I saw my first one . . .

—Linda J. Kulczyk

SKINWALKER IN ARIZONA

As half Navajo and Hopi, I've had my share of weird experiences on and off the Navajo and Hopi "rez." One experience that I would like to share happened when I was fourteen years old (I'm now twenty-nine). This is an experience that I have only shared with a small number of people. My brother, who is a hardened soldier, is still scared about what happened to us this particular evening. On with the story . . .

As a teenager, I would visit my grandma at her home on the Navajo rez for several weeks every summer. I loved to spend time with her, eat her delicious fried bread, and listen to her stories. Every so often my grandma would hire a worker, the harmless town drunk, to do odd jobs around her house and property. One evening right before the sun went down, I was asked by my grandma to take him home, which was about four miles out of the valley where she lived. I was more than happy to, seeing that I was only fourteen years old and was asked to drive a truck! Mind you, on the rez, nobody cares that you're only fourteen years old and driving around. Hell, there's hardly anybody around to see you anyway.

So my nine-year-old brother jumped in the truck cab with

me, the worker and my dog shared the tailgate of the truck, and we were off. After I dropped the worker off at the shack that he and his brothers called a house, we headed back down the road to our grandma's.

As I mentioned before, it was evening, and the sky was a deep red as the sun began to set behind us. We were leaving a nice dust trail from the dirt road, and the radio was playing music from the only radio station that could be picked up from the nearest town of Holbrook, Arizona.

Nothing seemed unusual, nothing felt weird. It was at this time that my eye caught movement of something in the bushes a little up the road to the right of us. I remember slowing down, thinking that it was one of the many free-roaming sheep in the area that would dart out in front of the truck. As I passed where I thought I saw it, I sped up thinking nothing else of it. Then, out of nowhere, I just felt this dark feeling of fear and dread. I had no idea why I was feeling this way, but I definitely felt that something was wrong.

As I play this memory back in my mind, there are only a few clear memories that I have of that evening. I clearly remember looking in my rearview mirror and seeing the dark silhouette of something very tall and very skinny that seemed to be covered with some kind of hair or fur running behind the truck after us! Whatever it was, it wasn't a normal human or human at all. I remember hearing my brother crying and my dog barking ferociously at whatever was chasing us. I remember speeding very fast and shaking violently as the truck bounced on the washboard dirt road. I distinctly remember that this thing was only getting closer as my brother cried, "It's coming up on your side!"

I remember being as scared as hell and thinking that I didn't want to die. At the moment that I thought would be our last, I remember speeding around a bend in the road and seeing a car coming toward us in the opposite direction. At that moment, I felt instant relief and felt that whatever was following us was gone.

Shaken up but alive, we made it to Grandma's house, wondering what the hell had just happened. We ran inside, not looking back, hoping that whatever was chasing us had not followed us home. As we told my grandma about our experience, she didn't seem too surprised, which surprised us. She responded by repeating stories that we had already heard at one point or another about black magic, witches, and something that the Navajos call *Yee Naaldlooshii*, or Skinwalkers. Needless to say, I didn't even want to look out any of the windows at all the rest of that night. As a matter of fact, I never drove again on the reservation at night until I was twenty-one years old.

Without going too deep into an explanation, I'll just say that these Skinwalkers are evil men and spirits that use black magic for evildoing. I tell you that as far-fetched as it may sound, they are real. I believe that if God and his greatness are real, the devil is equally as real and also has his ways of showing himself.

This may not sound very scary, and that may be due to my lack of writing skills. But what happened that evening really did happen and scared the wits out of me. I invite anybody to visit this part of Arizona if you have any doubt or want a huge scare. I promise you that you won't be disappointed.

—Lee Honawu

THE THING ON THE ROOF

I have been solo driving trucks for twenty years now. I have some really strange true stories. The most recent was while I was with Jim Palmer Trucking out of Missoula, Montana. I was going north on I–25 in Wyoming, maybe forty miles south of the Montana line. I stopped in a Wyoming rest area and cut off my truck. I had lain there for about twenty minutes, and I heard something land on my trailer. Well, it is one o'clock in the morning, what could it be? Not a bird, at one in the morning.

I did go out and check it; of course there was nothing. I was parked in the middle of the truck lot. No trees around to scrape my trailer. And there are no people here. These folks don't even have a vending machine to get a Pepsi. The truck lot is deserted. So I got back in the truck, got back in the sleeper, shut the light off, and tried to snooze, and I heard something banging down the top of the trailer, like it's walking on it. So I did this get-out-and-look thing several times, and also several times it sounded like someone was throwing rocks and hitting the side of the truck. So I think, maybe the birds are constipated? I don't know, and from what do birds get constipated? I mean, really. Like a horse getting lung cancer, you hear about that one all the time—right? So the birds, maybe too much fast food, too many chicken nuggets.

And so I got up and started the truck and put both fans on, the one in the cab and the one in the sleeper—full blast to drown out the sounds. But something landed on the roof. And it was heavy. Maybe landed as hard as a person, harder than a dog. But men don't fly, right? Or is this where the Superman stories come from? Maybe *some* kind of man-thing flies.

I have several true stories that are odd. I backpack by myself in the woods on my time off. And only in Arkansas have I ever gotten freaked out by two separate animals that I heard, that I have not ever heard anywhere else. One sounded like a hyena. (I checked the sounds they make on the Internet when I got back.) *But Arkansas doesn't have hyenas on the Ozark Highlands Trail.* And so now, when I hike the Ozark trail, I bring one of my guns—I like to be the one who lived to tell.

—Saraj Shea

A NOT-SO-GOOD NIGHT'S REST

About a year ago, a husband-and-wife team hauled a load of furniture to Steamboat Springs, Colorado, from Dallas, Texas. The furniture belonged to a family relocating to their dream home at Steamboat. The drivers received a call from the family on an incredibly beautiful Saturday morning to inform the drivers they were gonna be late getting to Steamboat as their car had broken down.

Unable to access the house to unload the furniture, the drivers figured they had all the time in the world to get to Steamboat from Denver. Never having been to Colorado before, they decided they would leave the truck stop in Denver and take a scenic drive to Steamboat via Rabbit Ears Pass and spend the night on top of Rabbit Ears, maybe take a short hike or something. It was an incredible October day, with crystal-clear skies and a light breeze. It was about sixty-two degrees as they left Kremmling, Colorado, for Rabbit Ears.

They found a parking spot along the highway on top of the pass. They noticed one other truck parked in that area, with its curtains drawn and the trailer's refrigerator running. To avoid the noise of the refrigerator, they pulled ahead another hundred feet or so and parked facing west. They watched the most wonderful sunset they had ever seen. They set up a couple of lawn chairs in front of their Kenworth to enjoy the evening. It got cold quick. Being natives of Texas, they got back into their truck to warm up and go to bed. The high altitude had its effect on them, and they went right to sleep.

About 2:00 A.M., the husband was awakened by the other truck starting up and leaving the parking area, making it extremely quiet. Shortly after that, he heard another truck with straight pipes throw on his jakes and begin his descent of the pass to the west, going toward Steamboat. He had just begun to doze when he felt the truck move, kind of like wind was blowing it sideways. But the wind wasn't blowing. He didn't get up and had begun to doze again when he felt the truck move again. This time it woke up his wife. "What was that?" she asked.

Shortly after that, the truck began to rock side to side, like someone had gotten a hold of the grab handles and was intentionally rocking the truck. Now the husband was a little shook up. He pulled on his pants so he could go kick the ass of whoever was messing with them. He threw open the curtains and looked out the window as he groped in the dark for his Maglite. He looked out of the passenger-side door—and noticed something big and dark looking back in at him. The thing looking in the window cocked its head. When his wife saw it, she screamed in terror.

"I was frozen," exclaimed the husband. "I didn't really know what I was looking at. Then it turned and walked away. It was tall enough to look straight in at us," he said.

The husband started up the truck, and they drove back to Steamboat. They don't want to even guess what it was they saw that night, for fear someone might call them crazy.

—Gary M. Vaughn

GHOST KISS

I have a story that happened to me a year or two ago while I was parked at a truck stop, sleeping in my truck bunk. I can't remember where this happened (state, city, etc.)—I wrote down the information in one of my many notebooks, and the notebook is in storage.

I am a female driver, and, at the time, I had my chow-shepherd-mix dog, Rowan, with me. We both sleep on the small bed. Rowan wanted to sleep at the head of the bed, so I turned around and put my head at what would be the foot of the bed. These truck beds are small, like twin size.

I was sleeping soundly when I was awakened by someone trying to kiss me. He was poking his tongue between my lips to try and get me to open my mouth a bit so he could kiss me. I remember an old boyfriend I had years ago that would do that. I kept my eyes closed because I thought that if I opened them, he would go away. This incident was a nice, sweet kiss and surely could have been a lot worse.

I decided to kiss him back. It was a sweet, regular kiss that a normal man and woman would exchange.

I am not that lonely on the road, as one might think. I have been single for about ten years by choice. I have my dog to keep me company, and my computer, audiobooks, podcasts, and work to keep me busy.

The way that this kiss happened was that, if this was a regular man in the cab with me, he would have had his back against the wall, and I would have had my back against a cabinet. And we would be very cramped. Rowan was taking up half the bed, so I was up against the wall, with only about a park-bench width to sleep on. When you are very tired, you can almost sleep anywhere, or in any position, I suppose.

So this man would have to have been *in the wall!* (as I was very close to the wall). With the amount of room I had to lay down, no regular man would have fit. We all three wouldn't fit on the bed: man, me, and dog! So he was actually "in the wall" and facing me.

It was very weird, and it was nice and sweet. I did not feel violated. It just felt more like a usual boyfriend kiss. That's my story.

—Susan Miller

DONNER SUMMIT

I've got just one story I can remember. I plow snow on I–80 over Donner Summit in California, and I work graveyard, 8:00 P.M. to 9:00 A.M. It was Sunday, and it had been a very long week, eighty-something hours straight already, so obviously I was in walking-zombie mode.

I was in my pickup driving to work at the time; it was a perfectly cold, crisp, and clear night. About ten miles from work, I realized that there wasn't a soul in sight on that interstate. Ten seconds after this thought, I suddenly got this vision of a person and his shadow running across the eastbound lanes then jumping over the K-rail (a temporary barrier) into the westbound lane right in front of me. I hit the brakes and locked them up, coming to a dead stop right in the middle of the number 1 lane. It was a good thing I did—someone *was* running across the road. But I seem to have missed him. I watched him run across the other two lanes and down the bank. My heart rate did not come down for at least a few hours. I remember this phenomenon every time I pass this spot driving at night.

—Hailey Petzoldt

HAT MAN ON THE MONTREAL AVENUE BRIDGE

It was a November night, already dark and cold, and fallen leaves scattered like insects as the car drove along. I was with my friend Elle, and we were taking a shortcut through Highland Park, to a restaurant known for their cookies-and-cream milkshakes. I took a left turn onto Montreal Avenue, at the base of a gradual but large hill. We were turning from the river road, which lined the Mississippi's lowland course eastward, into St. Paul, Minnesota. Even in the dark of the November night, the arched pedestrian bridge high above our heads, with wooded hills rising sharply on either side, almost seemed to mark a gateway to the higher ground ahead.

While certainly not one of the busiest arteries of traffic in the area, Montreal was still commonly used. The road ran upward like a ramp, with a large park and golf course straddling the road until the hill reached its crest, where the residential housing blocks began to mark the Highland Park sector of the city. I'd driven the route often enough, having a soft spot for chocolate cookies and vanilla ice cream, and it wasn't the first time Elle and I had made this trek together. This night was markedly different, however, and it wasn't just the spirit of the season playing tricks on us.

Almost immediately after passing through the doorway of the bridge, there was a distinguishable change in the tone of our car ride. It wasn't that I could have put my finger on anything in particular that happened, I was just suddenly and completely enveloped with a terribly heavy sense that something was wrong. I took my foot off the gas pedal, and, as the car began to slow, Elle reached over and turned down the radio. The car slowed to a crawl, and I pulled over to the right side of the road and turned to look at Elle. Her brows were furrowed as though she were listening for something.

"I don't know about you—" I began, but she quickly interrupted me.

"I know exactly what you're going to say, and I feel it too." We sat there for another second, listening to a few faint notes of the radio that were still audible. The park stretched away on both sides of the road, and, though it was dark, I could see the emptiness of landscape around us. It was only then I noticed that the street lamps lining the road were all out. It wasn't storming. In fact, it wasn't even windy, but we could clearly see across the expanses of browning grass, as our eyes were becoming accustomed to the dark. There wasn't a living creature in sight.

"Well . . . what should I do?" I finally asked.

"Just keep driving," she said, almost before I had finished my sentence.

I slowly pulled back into the lane, accelerating up the hill. It could have been the darkness, and it could have been the shift in the emotion of the atmosphere, but my heart was beating double time from the increased adrenaline in my system. The darkness that surrounded us was too thick, too complete.

"There isn't a single car on the road. There isn't a single car to be seen," Elle said, without moving her head. It was as though we just wanted to speed through and reach the top of the hill, and if we didn't move or breathe, we'd somehow get there faster. I made a quick scan with my eyes, making sure to check the rearview mirror. She was right, there weren't headlights anywhere around. Even on the shortcut, that just wasn't normal. Still, except for a bad feeling, there wasn't anything terribly out of place—until we saw *him*.

We were rolling up to the stop sign at the hill's peak when we noticed a man in the darkness, walking down the middle of the road. He was sauntering at a leisurely pace in the same direction we were driving, in a black trench coat and a black brimmed hat. He seemed unfazed by the approaching car lights, not moving at all. Indeed, not even turning to look at our approaching vehicle. I decided to ignore the stop sign.

"Oh, God, don't look at him," I heard Elle say as I watched her turn her face toward the passenger-side window. But I didn't need her to say that because I already instinctively knew not to do it myself. I looked to the lower right corner of the windshield as we passed him, and saw Elle crossing her arms over her stomach with my peripheral vision.

We rolled down the other side of the hill, residential houses and yards now standing vigil on the roadside—a reminder that we were becoming part of civilization once again. A streetlight shone before us, marking entrance back into the yellowed light of the city neighborhood. I distinctly remember fighting the urge to look in the rearview mirror.

Elle and I didn't speak a word until we were seated in a booth at the restaurant. It was clear we were both still plagued with the uncomfortable feeling that had started with that initial left turn.

"That was awful," I said to her, to break the silence. "Do you think we should tell someone?"

"Who?" she responded. "And besides, do you think anyone would believe us?"

—Rob Andrews

GHOST CAR IN THE GRAVEYARD

This just happened a month or so ago. I went to pick up my hubby from the train station in the little town where we live. He called while I was waiting and said he'd be a half an hour late. I was sitting in a heavy snowfall, so I drove across the street to the graveyard. The gravestones are old and big and looked pretty and interesting in the snow. While I waited, I thought I'd take some cool pics from inside the truck with the new camera that I bought for Christmas.

The graveyard is a maze of little roads, and the snow covered them deep. I drove slowly to scope out a good shot. I was way at the back of the graveyard and had stopped to take a few pictures when a car with no snow on it pulled up behind me. I felt a little ashamed for taking pictures of tombstones, so I quickly drove ahead to the next path that turned off the main pathway to let the car by. I turned into the path just enough so I could easily back out onto the main path, since the snow was deep and not plowed. I turned to look and see if the car had gone by me yet, but I saw no one—the car had vanished. I kept twisting around in my seat in all directions to see where the car went. But I couldn't see it anywhere.

I backed out on to the main path again and noticed that there was only one set of tracks in the snow. I turned the truck around to backtrack, thinking they must have turned off on a path I didn't see. But as I drove back, there was no path. I could see where I had been idling and no other tire tracks. I know there was a car behind me. I scanned the entire graveyard for this car while I drove back to the main road. On my way out to the street I never saw any tracks or signs of any other car.

I know there was a car; it was right on my bumper. Then it just disappeared. I got some nice shots that night in the graveyard, nothing but falling snow and tombstones. But I still wonder what the strange dark car was all about. I haven't gone back to the graveyard yet—but I will.

—Barbara Dexter

THE CROSS ON THE CAR

During my younger days in New York during the 1960s, my friends and I used to take turns borrowing our fathers' cars on a rotating basis (without their knowledge, not unlike many other guys). We would all get together and one of us would sneak his dad's keys. Then we would push the car out of the driveway very quietly, then down the street, where it was "anything goes" from there on out—as long as the car was home before dad woke up.

After a night of driving around Staten Island we would go home and coast the car into the driveway and no one was the wiser. We always had a good time until one night we decided to visit a cemetery at the end of a dead-end road.

There were four of us this night—nothing out of the ordinary. It was my turn to take my dad's station wagon. It was a fairly new Oldsmobile Vista Cruiser. It had no roof rack. (This is relevant to the story.)

We pushed the Vista Cruiser out of the driveway and down the street. Little did we know that this night wasn't going to be just another ordinary joy-riding experience.

It began just like any other night. Nothing special, and it was even getting boring just driving around. One of my friends suggested that we go to a graveyard. He just said a lot of cool things could happen in a cemetery. We figured it had to be better than what was going on, so we headed toward the river. On the way, one of the guys said he knew of this cemetery at the end of this old road. He gave the directions as we went. Sure enough, all by itself, at the end of this lonely road, was a very old cemetery.

I remember there was just one streetlight at the entrance, but the cemetery was dark. I drove up into the cemetery until the road ended. I am not sure why now, but everyone got out of the car except me. Maybe I was nervous, or maybe concerned for my dad's car. They were all acting goofy. You know how young guys act. A couple of the guys started acting like the *Night of the Living Dead*, climbing on my car, etcetera, until one of them broke my dad's rearview mirror off the car. That took the fun out of it for me, so I yelled for everyone to come back so we could leave and go to Wetson's for a burger at the other end of the island.

The guys came back to the car, and one was carrying a wooden cross. It was one of those temporary markers used for graves before the headstone is put on the grave. It was faded, dirty, and some of the paint was missing. The guy wanted to bring it with us, but everyone objected, saying it was bad luck. He held it by the end of the longest part below the cross and tossed it with a full swing into the darkness. Then he jumped in, and I backed the car out of the cemetery onto the road.

Now under the streetlight, the guys told me to burn rubber. I tried and tried but could not break the tires loose from the pavement. So everyone but me got out to lighten the load. I tried and tried but still couldn't. (It *was* a family station wagon.) I then drove up the street and backed up as fast as I could and threw it into drive, but the car would just come to an abrupt stop and stall. Now here is a very significant part—one of the guys saw an old tire and tried to put it on the roof to see if the car even had enough power to knock it off. I told him no, it would scratch the paint, and he dropped it. Well, the guys all got a big laugh about that. They all got back into the car, and we drove down by the river road. It was a winding road that went up the west side of the island. As we drove along, one of the guys suggested we stop by this closed bar he knew of. He said they threw away their empty kegs behind the bar and we could get a few.

So we went to the bar. I backed in, and two guys got out and started loading the kegs. I should have known that they were lying and the bar was open and a few kegs they took were full. Well, the bartender had seen or heard us. We took off, and now we had the bartender after us in his van. Racing down that winding road. Me screaming at them for lying to me and taking the kegs. Them rolling the kegs out of the back of the station wagon in front of the guy's van until the guy broke off the chase.

By now we are all excited, and I am very nervous and agitated. Just then someone yells, "Take a right!" So I slammed on the brakes and made a right turn onto a road with no houses. My friend said that he had been down the road a few days earlier and they had put down fresh tar to make repairs.

He suggested that I make one last try to spin the tires in the new tar. I drove for a little bit and he yelled, "There is the tar, STOP!"

I did. Being in the excited state that I was, I slammed on the brakes, and the car came to a full stop. Then, after the car came to a full stop, we all heard a scraping noise on the roof of the car and a bang on the hood. There, on the hood of my father's car, was the wooden cross that everyone had seen my friend throw away more than an hour before.

We had driven miles, made sharp turns, sudden stops, and drove quite erratically to evade the angry bartender. Yet the cross somehow held on? *Or did it?* I don't see how it could have, with a smooth roof and no roof rack. Also, the one kid had tried to put the tire on the roof and no one saw the cross then. Did it just get there somehow?

One of my friends was beside himself, very upset and yelling at us to get rid of it. The friend who originally found it swore he threw it away. And we all saw him do it. He said it was an omen and we should keep it. I got out of the car, took it off my hood, and gave it to him. We took it and talked about it the rest of the night. My one friend never was comfortable with keeping it.

We finally drove to the other side of the island that night to Wetson's. On our way back home, we got stuck driving behind another car. All of a sudden, in what seemed like slow motion, the entire area lit up, as bright as day but with a strange orange glow. Then there was an explosion louder than anything I have heard to this day. My dad's car and the car in front of us were pushed into the oncoming lane by the shock wave, and we both screeched to a halt. By now my one friend was really upset, saying that we should have never taken the cross.

Well, it wasn't the cross's fault, I don't think. It was a huge oil tank from a refinery in New Jersey that exploded. Talk about scary. We all went and watched the fire from across the river before going home. That ended our night of adventure. Our parents never knew.

Recently, I got hold of and talked to the friend who had taken the cross from the cemetery. I asked him one last time if he had put the cross on the car somehow. Forty years later he still swears he did not, explaining that even if he did, how would it have stayed on the car so long and no one saw it when they were out of the car a couple times. I had to agree that I had no explanation either.

Oh, and one last thing. Remember my friend who was so upset about the cross? It turned out that when the cross was cleaned and examined, the name on the cross was his grandmother's name . . . We talked about this for many years.

—Kim R. Kowalcyzk
Founder, The GhostBreakers
Paranormal Research Organization

RED-EYED MAN ON WISCONSIN HIGHWAY A

Never in my life have I been more terrified than I was that night in 2002. I was driving east on Wisconsin's Highway A, between Three Lakes and Sugar Camp. This highway was nothing out of the usual—it was quiet, the speed limit was 55 mph, and it had no history of hauntings.

It was a cool and dark spring night and the moon rose high. I was alone and just driving, thinking about things. The car radio was turned off. There's a stretch in the road that runs past an old building that served as a picnic house—the yard next to it had a park. I can't remember the last time I saw anyone there, or any kids. I was distracted and a little stressed out. I was looking at the old picnic house when I saw a figure in the middle of the road. I couldn't really make out what it looked like at that point. It was a man—at least it looked human. I swerved out of the way the moment I saw him, hitting the brake hard. I was nearly thrown into a ditch but came to an abrupt stop when I hit a tree, my car steaming, broken.

I was mad. Who wouldn't be? I got out of the car limping. My head was bleeding. I walked toward the figure, swearing at him.

"What the hell are you doing standing in the middle of the road, man!" I yelled.

The man had his back to me. He was wearing a trench coat and turned around to face me. This man's face was every scary movie you've ever seen—his face was white, his eyes red, glowing like fire. The best way to put it is that I was alone on a highway with a man who almost killed me, who had no face and red eyes.

His face was inhuman. It looked like it had been burned or like someone had thrown hot grease all over him. His face was so raw and frightening that I let out a scream of terror. The man opened his mouth and laughed like he heard a joke. His laugh was vibrant, bloodcurdling. What was even more bloodcurdling were the screams and moans he let out. I was beyond petrified. I ran, and he chased after me.

Soon his voice got closer and closer to me, which meant that he had to be getting closer and closer to me. The sounds that were coming out of him now sounded like he was crying and screaming and moaning at the same time. It was so high-pitched and loud at one point that I had to cover my ears. I could feel the man's breath on the back of my neck. Then the man grabbed me by the back of my neck.

I can't remember much after this. All I remember was seeing a light coming down the road and turning into two lights. I heard beeping, and then I fell down, while that terrifying scream echoed in the back of my head. I saw a figure coming up to me and heard them yell at someone to call an ambulance.

I woke up in the hospital. My head and legs hurt. A nurse came up to me and said something that I couldn't hear. I just heard barely audible sounds and moans from somewhere. Then my parents came.

I stayed another night in the hospital, and my hearing didn't come back for another two days. All I could think about was what I saw the night before, and I was still afraid.

My hearing loss was obviously caused by whatever that creature was that kept crying and screaming into my ears. My parents told me that when they came to see me I was as white as snow.

In the daytime, about a month later, I went back to the highway with my friend. We saw the remains of my car, which had been taken to the dump a couple of weeks earlier. We came to the spot where I had encountered the red-eyed man and walked around a little bit. We went around the park and through the woods. My friend almost couldn't believe what I had told him. But he did believe that something bad happened to me that night.

I don't know who the red-eyed man was, why he was chasing me, why he was screaming, why he had red eyes, why his face was all messed up, why he was in the middle of the road . . . I don't know anything. I just know that I don't drive on that highway at night anymore.

—Logan Lee Braasch

APPARITION IN ARKANSAS

My adoptive mom has experienced some horrific hauntings, ghosts, and spirits. This incident happened about a year ago.

My mom called me one afternoon, in a frantic state. What she told me brought chills to my whole body. She was traveling on a road in Arkansas when a herd of deer ran out in the middle of the road at 9:36 P.M. The traffic went from 70 mph to *brakes!* There were two eighteen-wheelers in front of her, and three cars in front of them. So you can only imagine the outcome. The eighteen-wheelers had to stop so quickly that the trailers swung around and cleared everything within their path, including the cab of her truck. Wreckage and deer were strewn all over the road.

Luckily, my mom was able to stop just in time, due to the safe distance that she kept between her and the vehicle ahead of her. (She has driven a truck for twenty years.) As she pulled off the median, she noticed a man standing six feet from her trailer. She wondered how a man got next to her trailer so fast and without her seeing him. She said the man had one hand across his chest and one hand in his pocket, and looked very confused.

The rescue team was on the way while the police were investigating the accident. One officer walked up to my mom and asked, "What happened here?"

As she was telling him about what happened, she mentioned that "someone needs to check this guy out back by my trailer. He looks very confused, he might wander off in the traffic."

The cop said, "What man?"

Well, he was just there, in plain view! The officer got a detailed description, down to facial hair and shoes. He walked away for a minute, then came back. He said, "The man you described is the owner of that wrecked eighteen-wheeler and was found dead at the scene." My mom was in shock as the cop just turned around and walked the other way.

After she left, my mom stopped at a truck stop. The TV was on, and a news station was covering the wreck she had just witnessed. There were four fatalities that night. My mom had left the scene before the rescue team came. The man she had seen next to her truck was one of the victims in the accident.

—Sandy F. Bower

GRAVITY HILL

Some seven-eight years ago, when I was a small boy, I used to go on trips with my dad, who is an OTR (over-the-road) driver in Europe. (I am from Estonia.) We were heading home through Slovakia, which is pretty mountainous. As we were driving up and down the hill, at one point my father discovered that the truck's performance was not what it should be. We could hardly get 60 kph (35 mph) down the hill (the truck was a Volvo FH12 semi with 420 horsepower). Our first thought was that the brakes were jammed on. We went out to inspect if any of the brakes were abnormally hot. Some were a bit hot, but that is normal in hills, as you know.

We got back into the cab, and, as my dad released the parking brake, we noticed that our fully loaded semi (forty tons) was rolling backward *up* the hill. Neither of us said a word for a minute. Our next thought was that maybe there is some very weird fault in the transmission. To exclude that possibility, my dad shut down the engine and—surprise, surprise—the truck was still rolling uphill. The "force" ended after driving us about three to five miles. We told the story to other truckers later. Nobody believed us and thought we were confused which way was up and which way was down the hill. Unfortunately, at this time cell phones with cameras were not yet popular or in masses (at least in our country), and we couldn't film it.

Other things that my father has seen: Two suns (but this should not be paranormal; I have read recently that it has something to do with atmosphere temperatures and can be seen, though rarely). And, back in the nineties, when my dad was driving between Finland and Russia, one night in Moscow he saw a flying object that traveled abnormally fast. It could not have been a falling star because it made ninety-degree turns instantly.

—Gert Vatt

WEIRD LIGHT IN TORONTO

Back when my wife and I were dating, in the first few months, we were out on a date. She lived on the outskirts of Toronto, so it was kind of suburban. You could see lots of bright stars and not a lot of light from urban areas. The sky was pretty clear.

We were parked in back of this school; in the backseat; and, let's just say, getting to know each other. And out of the corner of her eye, she kept looking through the window and beyond me. I was twenty years old at the time, and I'm like, what are you looking at?

And she said, "There's a weird light over there." So I looked over my shoulder and between two apartment buildings, but way out into the distance, maybe a couple of kilometers away, I saw this big bright light. It looked like a streetlight basically, but way up high, too high for a streetlight, but it had that sort of characteristic.

So I said, "It's a streetlight, who cares?" And this kept going on for twenty minutes or so. She kept looking up at the light. But she knew the area—it was her neighborhood; I didn't know the area. The light was stationary; it wasn't moving.

She kept looking at it and I said, "Okay, stop now, c'mon!"

And then she said, "But it moved! Did you notice that it moved? It was in a different spot before . . ."

I thought, what are you talking about? So I looked out the window, and, sure enough, it had moved. I had looked over my shoulder half a dozen times before to see it because she kept looking at it. When we saw it, it was stationary again, but instead of being between the two buildings, it had moved a little bit lower and to the right. And it had been in one spot for the first twenty minutes.

I thought, okay, that's kind of weird. And the second we got out of the car and closed the door, it started moving. So it had been in the same spot for maybe twenty minutes and then in the next spot for maybe fifteen minutes; then, when we got out of the car, this thing just started moving, fast! And it was getting closer, and pretty low to the ground. And it was coming over to us, and we were looking at this thing—at this point, I was frozen. You start thinking to yourself, well a plane doesn't hover, so it can't be a plane. Meanwhile, it was still getting closer. Then I started thinking, oh, maybe it's a helicopter, like a police helicopter. But as it got closer, I saw it was *big*. And helicopters make noise—this was completely silent.

So now it was coming toward us directly. And as it came closer, it sort of came horizontally toward us. So we turned our bodies to watch it cut across us (rather than toward us). And we were staring at it. At this point, it was pretty close. It wasn't a plane up in the sky; it wasn't a helicopter; it wasn't a satellite; it wasn't a comet. And it *flew*. When it was coming toward us, we couldn't really judge the depth of field, but it seemed to be coming at us at about the speed of a plane.

But as it came closer to us, as it came across our vision, it became clearer what it was—sort of an oval sphere, a spheric source of light, orange and yellow. It had no wings; it was just light, one blur, basically. The object itself was a light. And it went really fast, right past us.

So now, we looked over to the right, and it stopped again. It's stationary again. It was at about a forty-five-degree angle to the right of us. And it stayed still again for about another ten to fifteen seconds—then it sort of blinked a couple times and took off, and we couldn't see it anymore.

My wife and I don't talk about it. Every time I tell people, she says, don't tell that story! And I'm like, why? She says people will think we're crazy. But I don't care. My philosophy is basically this: I do believe in ghosts and spiritual things like that, but I'm not a big alien guy. I don't really believe in aliens—well, I'll leave it like this: I don't know. I don't know what this was. I don't know if it was a UFO. (I guess it was a UFO, because it was unidentified.)

All I know is, I know what it wasn't. It wasn't a plane; it wasn't a helicopter; it wasn't a satellite; it wasn't a comet. It was too close to be anything from the universe and too far to be something that was being propelled from the earth. We don't know what it was. That's the whole point—we just don't know what it was.

—George Phillips

ALIEN DRONE AT THE POTATO HARVEST AND OTHER STRANGENESS IN COLORADO

I'm the proprietor of the UFO Watchtower in Hooper, Colorado, which is located in Colorado's San Luis Valley. In 2008 there were an abundance of daytime sightings all over the valley. People were reporting them from everywhere. Now UFO sightings happen all the time around here. The strange thing about these sightings is that the UFOs were silver balls.

I had a fella drop by the UFO Watchtower who was employed at the Las Alamos National Lab in New Mexico. He, too, had seen the silver balls so asked his supervisor about them. The supervisor told him that they were drones just checking us out.

The one I got to see was when I was working the potato harvest in late September. We were sitting on the back of the truck having lunch when I saw a commercial jet flying from east to west. A silver ball appeared behind the jet and was bouncing up and down on the jet stream like it was playing at an amusement park. I yelled at the guys, "Do you see that? Do you see that?" Hell, they couldn't see the plane, let alone the silver ball, and then they had the utter gall to tell me I was crazy and seeing things . . . go figure!

The following year, on August 28, 2009, my partner, Stan, and

I made a trip to Denver from the San Luis Valley to see my dad and my stepmother, Verna. Stan doesn't like to drive with lots of traffic, so he always insists upon leaving between 4:00 and 4:30 A.M. (I didn't even know that those god-awful hours existed until I got tied up with him!)

We were traveling north on Highway 17 and were at about F Road (four or five miles from the house) when I saw something about a thousand feet in the air crossing in front of us. I pointed it out to Stan, but he seemed oblivious to the idea that something abnormal was going on and didn't say a word or pay attention to the object. I rolled my window down but heard nothing.

It was still pitch-black out. The object was dark-colored and wasn't moving very fast. What was really strange was it had lights (green, amber, and white) that were circling around it. It was traveling from the west to the east, and I could no longer see the lights once it was about a mile or so away. As always, I tried to rationalize what the object was. Not a helicopter, no noise whatsoever; definitely not a weather balloon; too slow for a plane; and, again, not loud enough. What type of object would have lights encircling it and no noise? A UFO?

In the San Luis Valley, UFO sightings are not considered unusual. There have been documented sightings since the sixteen hundreds, when the Spanish explorers documented the strange phenomenon. There have also been many cattle mutilations (it is estimated ten to fifteen thousand since the 1960s, when the infamous Snippy the horse was mutilated on a ranch near Mount Blanca, Colorado). What I can't understand is why mutilations weren't publicized prior to the 60s . . . didn't hear about them prior to that.

I saw an animal that had been mutilated, and it was bizarre— not so much the cuts and other injuries, but the behavior of the other cattle. The cow had a calf, but the calf would not go near her, which is highly unusual. (We've had cows that have died, and their calves still won't leave their mama's side). The other cows made a big circle around the mutilated cow (about twenty of them), and one by one would take a step forward and jump back, step forward and jump back. Just not typical.

The rancher told us that the day before the mutilation, military aircraft were flying over the pasture. Now figure that one out. But it's not unusual to have reports of black helicopters in the area where there's been a mutilation.

This entire phenomenon is not scary to me but interesting. I want to know more and see more and meet "them." I feel that if "they" were the monsters as they are portrayed in the movies, then why haven't they done away with us humans? And why haven't they taken over our planet since their technology is so much greater than ours is? I have never experienced anything negative with the UFO phenomenon, only good.

—Judy Messoline
Owner of the UFO Watchtower

STRANGE CLOUD OVER HIGHWAY 50

I was living in Red Wing, Minnesota, and worked in Minneapolis when this happened. I was going to work about 5:15 A.M. on Highway 50. The sun wasn't up yet—but in the sky, there were all these low, puffy gray clouds. And right in front of me came down a typical silver disk, what you would, you know, hear about. It had really large round windows, like circles, with a dark line on the inside of the circle. I could see about four of them. And they looked to be about five to six feet across. And then on top of it were smaller circles. And they weren't symmetrical; they were asymmetrical. I just saw a curve of the disk. It came down right in front of me. And I looked at it for like ten seconds—with my mouth open. And then it just went back up in the cloud.

There was a pickup to my left, and a small car behind me. I don't know if they saw it or not, because I tell you I was so shocked I didn't even look over. I was just thinking, I wish I had a camera in my eye. 'Cause I could fumble in my purse and look for my cell phone and try and take a picture. And by then it would have been gone.

It was amazing. It was right in front of me, and it was *huge*. And I drove to work with my mouth hanging open almost the whole time, 'cause that's the closest I've ever come to a UFO.

—Mary Lou

GHOST MAN IN MICHIGAN

Back in early fall 2008, my wife and I were making a trip to southwest Michigan to visit friends. They live roughly twenty minutes north of South Bend, Indiana, in what is best described as a very remote and sparsely populated area. Our friends live on a dark road that, a mile or so beyond their house, turns into a gravel drive.

My wife and I live in Ohio and both work full-time, so by the time we arrived in southwest Michigan, it was nighttime. This was a trip we made many times, but this particular night was very different. The road is full of blind turns, thick woods, and wild animals, especially deer. So, needless to say, that night we were driving cautiously and were on the lookout for deer that might dart out onto the road. To make matters worse, there was a light fog hugging the ground.

As we neared our friends' house, out of the corner of my eye, I noticed what appeared to be a gentleman standing in the weeds / tree line. He was standing still, staring out onto the road. He was wearing a flannel shirt and overalls, but I remember that I couldn't see the lower part of his body below his knees. And he wasn't fully solid . . . he had a hazy white look. As I drove by, there was dead silence in the car. A few seconds passed, and I turned to my wife to ask her if she just saw something. When I looked into her eyes and saw the expression on her face, I knew she saw what I saw. We could not explain it but know that it was something paranormal.

There are a lot of wetlands and bogs in that area of Michigan. The Mud Lake Bog Nature Preserve is extremely close to where we saw the man. (I have heard that bodies of water and moisture in the air may help enhance paranormal activity.) Every time thereafter that we have driven past that spot on the road, we get the same tingly sensation we felt the night when we saw the ghostly man in overalls.

—Dan Kopec

TWO DEAD RABBITS

I'll not forget one hot early afternoon drive in a rig hauling Rocklite from near Trona, California, to a plant near Temecula. It was July 1956. Back on the paved road, heading south toward Red Mountain, the slightly overloaded Peterbilt combination was doing well at about fifty. No air-conditioning in that tractor made these trips uncomfortable, and the twenty-mile corduroy dirt road to the quarry site added to my dread of taking this haul.

Something running into the road ahead caused me to quickly slow down. A man suddenly stopped nearly in the center of the road, waving his arms wildly. I braked to a stop just short of him. His wild hair blew in the hot desert wind. He had no shirt, dirty khaki pants, and his bare feet looked like old dust-covered shoes. He seemed to be dangerously sunburned. He approached my driver's-side door and climbed up onto the running board, his face and eyes as wild looking as his hair.

"What's the matter?" I asked.

He couldn't seem to answer at first. He was breathing as if he'd run a marathon. Sweat and dirt coated his blistered face, and his lips were cracked from the sun. He seemed to be in a panic about something. Short of forcing him into the cab for a trip to a hospital, all I could think of was my lame question.

"I asked what's the matter. You need help? Can I take you somewhere? You look like you need medical help."

"No! No!"

"Why did you stop me?"

He pointed over the hood of my tractor about northwest and exclaimed, "There are two dead rabbits out there! There are two of 'em! They're dead! Rabbits! There are two dead rabbits out there!"

Figuring he was a heatstroke victim and hallucinating, I was at a loss as to what to do. "Let me pull over and we'll go see what you're talking about. I've got a jug of water. How about some water?"

"No! No water! They're way out there. Two dead rabbits." With that he climbed down from the running board, crossing in front of my rig to the other side of the road, and headed off on a faint trail through the desert scrub. I called to him, but he didn't heed my call. He just kept walking as if he knew where he was going.

Heading back south toward 395, my conscience began to work on me. Sorting through various possibilities, from "I could have forced him to get help" to "He's not my problem," I ended up driving my load to its destination near Temecula. In order to at least do something, I called the San Bernardino County sheriff's office and told them of the incident, giving the time, his description, and the location south of Trona, as best I could. No cell phones, CB radios, or GPSs in those days.

But that sweaty, wild-eyed, cracked face, a foot away from me at my driver's-side window, screaming at me, haunted me for years. I can still envision that frantic man and "hear" his alarming announcement about those two dead rabbits. My imagination makes me wonder if he'd seen two human bodies somewhere out there in the sand. For years, especially if I heard the theme to *The Twilight Zone*, his image and declaration, "There are two dead rabbits out there," came to mind. I never did find out what really happened out there in the desert, but I believe that there is more to this story than two dead rabbits.

—Christopher Rubel

ETs IN NORTH CAROLINA

My father was a truck broker; my grandfather was a farmer. I began riding in trucks when I was three years old, going from Florida to South Carolina from my parents' home to my grandparents' home. We followed the crops all the way up the East Coast and sometimes into Canada in the fall so that my father could work and load the trucks. At age eighteen, I had a chauffeur's license, and I kept the chauffeur's license until the CDL (commercial driver's license) came in, and I decided that, rather than being grandfathered in, I would just not drive the truck anymore.

I drove most of the time with my husband in the 1970s and 1980s, and we drove coast to coast. We'd start in Florida and drive to LA, maybe have another stop in San Francisco or San José, load something up there—strawberries or lettuce, or whatever we could get—and take it back to the East Coast (usually to Philadelphia, sometimes to Atlanta). Sometimes we would haul plants out of Half Moon Bay, California, and have thirty or forty drops. I did a lot of trucking, probably half a million miles myself.

I've had a lot of experiences, whether or not they were paranormal, I don't know. I used to see a lot of lights in the sky playing, and I considered them to be flying saucers because they would jump around and disappear and they went so fast that there was no way they could be regular airplanes of any kind. I saw this while taking the southern routes on either Interstate Highway 20 or 10, going through the deserts of New Mexico, Nevada, Arizona, and west Texas.

I did have a direct encounter with the lights going to Iowa one time. There was a light in the sky that tracked us. We had to pull over on the side of the road and lost about four hours of time—we woke up back in the vehicle on the side of the road, going "What time is it? What just happened?" We didn't have any recollection of what had happened, no memory of what we had experienced. We have had vague partial recollections of the time-loss experience surface years later that are disconcerting—nothing concrete, just vague, half-formed memories that are uncomfortable, usually brought to mind by a smell, a sound, a metallic taste, or perhaps a flash of light. When I add up all the bits and pieces, the story becomes more complete and more confusing at the same time.

We were on the way to the truck one time, and we saw a small ship on the side of the road. It was about three feet across and had a little antenna on the top. It was on four legs and had lights going around the middle. This was out in North Carolina, where I lived, on a dirt road that we lived on, on the side of the mountain. We parked our truck at the foot of the mountain and were coming down in the car (to get the truck) when we saw it. I tried to get out, but my husband reached across the seat and said, "I don't think that's a good idea—we're outta here." When we came back, of course, it was gone.

I have had direct contact with alien beings while living on the mountain. They left about two years ago—I have no idea why—but they were here for probably ten or twelve years. They were short, like little Greys, only they were rounder. I think there are different species, different groups that come from different places. I think some are really good and some are really nasty, just like humans. Some are just mischievous—they're not going to hurt you, they just want to mess with you. That's what the ones up here were like.

I think there are a lot of them here, but as far as the mountain I live on, there is a federal aviation tower on top and all kinds of antennae, and all sorts of questionable goings on underneath. It's a government facility, and I think ETs are attracted to those. I think it's possible that the government and the ETs are working together in some instances. Maybe that's where we've gotten some of our technology.

—Rebecca

TURNPIKE TO THE TWILIGHT ZONE

I t was early November of 1979. I had just moved back to my hometown of Pittsburgh from the Colorado Rockies. On a gray Sunday afternoon I was bored and restless and decided to catch a movie at the local theater about a mile or so away.

I looked up at the sky as I got out of my car several blocks from the movie house. Overhead, the soggy graphite clouds were ready to burst. If it was raining when the show let out, I'd be sopping wet and freezing cold by the time I got back to my Olds station wagon. I didn't wear a jacket.

A few hours later as I left the theater, I saw a major cloud burst looming just seconds away in the dark swirling skies above me. I made a dash for my car, jumped in, and closed the door just as the rain fell in buckets and my wipers began to flap back and forth. In the deluge, they were all but a formality as I began the slow crawl home.

Although I hadn't been in town for several years, I knew exactly where I was. Go down this street, make a left, follow a mile and . . . *wait* a second. I must have made a wrong turn in this crazy storm. I am now heading down a long, steep road I have never seen before. I look for a place to turn around, but none appears. So I just keep going farther down this weird winding road that looks like it is in the middle of the country, not the urban neighborhood I just left with its delis and chain pharmacies.

Finally, I saw a turnoff fifty feet before me. I look at the sign. The name of the street wasn't familiar, but I calculated that it would take me back in the direction I wanted to go. Yet the farther I went down this road, the stranger I started to feel. Nothing seemed even remotely familiar in a way that is hard to describe. Every city has its own look and feel. Los Angeles simply doesn't look like Cincinnati. And this didn't look like Pittsburgh. *I guess it's just an area I haven't been to before . . .*

After five minutes of driving through lord knows where, I banged the steering wheel and started to curse. But my anger was almost fake—more of a nervous reaction. I was not angry at being lost. I was secretly freaked out at being—no—I was *lost.* That's all it was. I was lost.

At this point I had the existential realization that when you're "normally" lost you have *some* idea of where you are. The city, anyway. But right then, if I had the guts to admit it to myself, I would have had to say I am somewhere far, far away.

The sun comes out. It is now a sparkling blue sky. I look up at the brilliant sun. Boy, *that* was quick.

I drove for fifteen minutes. Twenty minutes. Thirty. Nothing looked even remotely familiar anymore. At that point I was laughing and making half-insane crude remarks as road signs read names I knew were not from the area.

Eucalyptus Avenue! Why, of course! Lots of fricking eucalyptus in Pittsburgh. Now I know exactly where I am—by the ocean!

Jesus H. Christ. This is insane. *I mean,* in-sane.

Then, Eureka! A sign for the turnpike! *Oh, thank you almighty God in heaven. THANK YOU!* I knew the Pennsylvania Turnpike like the back of my hand. To get home all I needed to do was find exit 7, and no matter where in bleeding hell I was now, I'd be home in fifteen minutes—once I found exit 7.

Thank you, exit 7, wherever you are.

I pulled up to the on-ramp of the turnpike. Hmm. That's interesting. There. Is. No. One. In. The. Tollbooth.

Empty. I looked behind me. No cars. I was going to ask the attendant where I was. But. . . .

"Sweet *mother . . .*" I swore under my breath as I pulled up to the tollbooth.

But, hey, no big deal. It's automated! That's why there was no one there.

I took my ticket from the automated machine. Drove onto the turnpike. And looked at the card. Um, where is exit 7? Where. Is. Exit. 7? It's not on the card. And the names of the exits, the cities, *what are these? Jamesburg? Hunh!?!? Where am I, Maryland??* And as I drove down what I realize now is a brand-new turnpike, I also noticed something else: *there are no cars on it.* Not *one* going either way. Brand-spanking-new turnpike. Completely empty. For miles and miles.

Then I realized, *Oh, shit! I am on a new turnpike that isn't meant for traffic yet!?!?* I drove for ten minutes. Miles and miles of two-lane, perfectly paved, brand-new empty turnpike. Fifteen minutes. Still no cars.

So now I realized I had to turn around. I know it's a huge fine, but what else was I supposed to do? I find a crossover, make the U-turn, and start preparing my story to tell the tollbooth guy—assuming he was just away on a pee break or sumthin' and will be there when I get back.

Dum de dum dum dum. I looked out at the miles and miles of empty turnpike. *Why are they building a brand-new turnpike anyway? This must cost gazillions! We already have a turnpike, for chrissakes. Oh, here is the exit. OK, prepare the story . . .*

But, uh, nope. Nobody at the tollbooth. In fact, the toll gate is up.

I drove through. *Oh, thank you! No $375 fine!*

OK, now. Make a left or a right? I made a left. And then, after only a minute or so, there it is, a road I know! It shouldn't be here, thirty minutes from where I started, but what the hell? I know this road. My relief almost brings me to tears. And the road took me home.

"How was the movie?" my mother asked as I walked in the kitchen.

"Oh, uh, it was okay. But, man, you would not believe how lost I got! I didn't know they were building a new turnpike. I was on that thing for twenty minutes. Not one car! It was *bizarre.*"

My mother furrowed her brow. My dad smiled.

"What? Isn't there a new turnpike?"

"I don't think so," my mother said.

"No. Not that I've heard of," my dad said. They looked at me blankly. Knowingly. Like I just unwittingly admitted I'd been smoking some serious pot over the past few hours.

For days afterward I asked around. Nope. No new turnpike.

Fifteen years later I was at a conference in Los Angeles where the speaker, Carlos Castaneda, electrified us with one of his outlandish tales of sorcery.

"One day, Taisha was driving," he says. "We were driving down Alhambra when we look around and suddenly, *Poof!* We don't know where we are! We drove into another world!" he smiles broadly, barely able to contain himself. "I tell you: be careful when you drive down steep, winding roads like this one," he cautions. "Apparently, once a great river flowed down this road. But now, even though it has long since dried up, the great energy of the river still flows here and can take you away!"

Everyone in the audience giggles nervously at his silly story. I laughed too, when something abruptly takes me back.

I remember the steep, winding road. The ghost turnpike. The shuddering realization of being lost in another world.

From fifty feet away Carlos turned from the crowd and imperceptibly pointed a finger at me, smiling.

"He knows," he said quietly, raising his eyebrows playfully.

I continued to live in Pittsburgh and still do to this day, but it was many years before I had reason to be back in the neighborhood where "the event" first unfolded. Something about the area, the street, continued to impart a disturbing mood in me. As though I couldn't be anywhere near that theater without feeling I was standing on the high dive for the first time. Looking down. Knowing it was too late to turn back.

Then, one afternoon, a strange urge came over me. Almost like I was hypnotized. And I found myself driving my car right to the corner of the avenue where I had parked those many years ago. I casually looked over like I was at my twenty-year reunion facing the bully who had tormented me in high school. And I got a chill when I saw the name of the street. Forward Avenue. As though it truly is an otherworldly launch pad that thrusts you forward and out of this world into who knows where?

—R. Dustin Mercer

ALIEN ENCOUNTER AT DEACON'S CORNER TRUCK STOP

This experience occurred in 1987—on August 9, 1987, off of Highway 1. There's a truck stop called Deacon's Corner just south of Winnipeg, Canada. It's kind of a famous truck stop, but I didn't know that until quite a bit later. Highway 1 is the major highway in Canada. It goes from the east coast to the west coast. And Deacon's Corner is kind of like the center of that particular highway.

I pulled in about one or two in the morning. I was driving a 1987 Honda Civic, which, of course, was quite a small car to be parked in the lot at a truck stop. And I was exhausted. I had driven almost eleven hours, and I pulled in to try and get a little bit of sleep—I thought that the truck stop might afford me the opportunity to do that.

But I was never able to really get to sleep, as the trucks kept coming into the area, at least for the first thirty minutes or so that I was in the car. I was getting upset because I thought another truck was pulling in, and it was getting way too close to my car. The truck lights were blasting right into the car. When this transport truck was up really close, it was like someone shining a big spotlight at the car. With my eyes closed to shelter them away from the intense light, I thought, "Hold on a second; I don't hear his engine." Then the lights slowly moved over the top of me. I immediately realized this wasn't a transport truck or a plane or any common mechanical device. I could make out that the lights were multicolored. Some were red, blue, orange—most of them were white.

I had stretched out on the passenger side of the vehicle to move the pedals out of the way and get more comfortable as I tried to sleep. Now, with this object over the car, the air had suddenly gone dead . . . there was no echo in the air. It was as if the density of the air had changed, like the physical characteristics and properties were different. That's the only way I can describe it, "dead air." No sound transmission; there was no sound coming from anything. It's very difficult to explain to someone who hasn't experienced it.

When the lights moved over the vehicle, I had become nearly completely paralyzed. I could breathe but could not move any of my limbs. I couldn't move to get out of the car. Just before the object moved over the vehicle, I could hear the engine of another truck that had pulled in behind my vehicle. It blocked the view of the people in the restaurant that was about thirty meters away. Nobody in the restaurant was going to be able to witness what was happening, and I had no idea where the driver of the truck behind me was or what was he seeing. Was he experiencing this incredible paralysis? Was he struggling like me to get out of his cab? Was he screaming for help?

And then a few things happened very quickly. I remember all the hairs on my arms stood on end just as if I was in an intensely powerful electromagnetic field. I just assumed that whatever this craft was, its propulsion system was generating this field of energy. I tried to keep my eyes closed for most of it because it was so terrifying. I was worried about what I was being exposed to. It seemed likely this was a UFO, and I sure didn't want to see anything nonhuman. I wasn't sure how I would react, and I didn't want to panic and do something stupid that might jeopardize my life. This experience was a hundred-percent real, and it was going to take all my emotional, mental, and physical strength to get through this. In the next agonizing seconds, I was pulled on board the craft.

I found myself with four or five distinctly nonhuman beings in front of me. They were dressed in beige jumpsuit uniforms. They were all about similar height, around four feet high, somewhere in that neighborhood. They're very similar in structure to what people claim are the Greys, but there were some stark differences. Their skin color was off-white, kind of like a milky white. It was darker than our skin color, but I wouldn't say it was gray. Their eyes were very large, and they weren't completely black; they actually had pupils. And their eyes were a brilliant blue—all the beings I saw had the same haunting, beautiful, and piercing eyes. They had no hair, very slender noses with very slender mouths, and only holes for ears.

Their skulls looked slightly bi-lobed. I noticed when I was walking behind one that there was a pulsation, and I could actually see some of the veins in its head. I can't remember what their hands and feet looked like. I think I was just staring at their heads and their eyes. One of the things that struck me was that their neck structure looked way too small to support the size of their heads. Their necks were probably no more than three or four inches in diameter, which would mean their physiology was something very different from ours. Their heads were twice the size of ours.

When I was initially taken on board and opened my eyes, I actually staggered against an object on my left, and I took a quick glance, and it was my car. They had somehow managed to take me and my car on board this craft! One minute I'm in the passenger's seat; and then they moved me through the windshield of the car. I don't know how they did that. That process actually hurt. There was a lot of pain and discomfort associated with getting moved into the ship. And I was scared.

Being scared, I got angry. I think that's just a natural response when you're faced with something that you're not prepared for. I mean, prior to this experience the only thing I ever knew about extraterrestrials was probably what I saw on *Star Trek*. I assumed that, yeah, there probably are extraterrestrials out there in the universe. Maybe they even look pretty much like us, or are pretty much like us. But nothing really could have prepared me for the experience, the raw . . . I'll call it the raw reality of the experience that I was faced with.

I was angry with the beings. I started yelling and swearing at them, saying, "You don't have the right to do this! What do you guys think you're doing?" Part of me was afraid they were gonna hurt me again. I yelled, "You know, you could have used the f'ing door!"

And one stood up and said, "What do you need doors for?"

The question stunned me. I thought, "How do I answer that? How can I even start to explain why I need to use the door?" Like I'm thinking, "How in the world am I gonna communicate with these guys if we don't even have doors in common?" I continued to get more angry and indignant, when another being stepped forward, and . . . *zap!* I was completely calm. They had the ability to influence my emotional state and calm me down. I don't know how they did that, but they did, and immediately I was calm. And this being said, "Come with me."

And I said, "Okay." It seemed a natural thing for me to do, and I just followed without a question and without anger. This was of course very bizarre behavior considering the circumstances. Everything that they suggested to me I felt was the right thing to do. What was also remarkable about this experience is that they spoke perfect English. I didn't pick up an accent from them at all. I don't understand, but it suggested to me that these beings are well aware of our culture. They certainly made a tremendous attempt to try to understand it, and even understand the language. So this was not telepathic communication. They spoke English to me, and they only spoke it in very short sentences of two to five words. That's the maximum. They didn't go into long explanations or orations. They just told me to do something, and I just went ahead and did it. They said, "Come with me," and I went with them, and those types of things. But they didn't speak English to each other. They seemed to just know what to do and went ahead and did it.

As the experience continued, I underwent a number of medical procedures. And I blacked out. I'm not sure why I blacked out.

Maybe it was because of the pain or something that was occurring to me in one of the procedures. At the end of these procedures, I had found myself regaining consciousness on a table. And there were two large beings, very similar in structure to all the other beings that I'd seen, but they were dressed in black uniforms—and they were about ten feet tall.

I had never seen any living thing on two legs that was this large. I was still just waking up, just in a fog, trying to get my bearings as to where I was and what was going on around me. There were other beings that were around me, dressed in white lab coats. They stepped away from the table and then another being stepped forward—she was about 5'3", 5'4", somewhere in that neighborhood. She's slightly taller than the other, smaller beings, but obviously quite a bit shorter (about half the size) of those two beings that were at the edge of the table.

I assumed the ten-foot-tall beings at the edge of my table were kind of like soldiers or guards, in a sense. They were watching to see what was going to happen. They then proceeded to kind of release some control over me. And one of the beings came toward me and said, "We don't understand your anger." This struck me as very odd, as I was still trying to get a sense of where I was and what was still going on around me, and, you know, if this nightmare was going to continue or not. I still wasn't sure whether or not I was going to get out of this whole experience alive.

When I've played sports in the past and found myself in difficult situations, I've always reasoned and rationalized to myself that, "You know what? Try and find out what's going on, and don't panic if you don't have to." My rationale was to develop some kind of communication with them and figure out what they were doing, who they were, what they wanted with me and to convince them to let me go.

And the being said again, "We don't understand your anger." The statement felt like it was coming from a mannequin. I was trying to read her reactions or emotions but couldn't perceive any emotions at all. It was very clinical and impossible to interpret. I then thought she must be referring to when I came on board. I wanted to say, "I'm sorry. I just wasn't expecting it to hurt and that is why I was angry!" But all I managed to say was, "I'm sorry . . . ," and this emotional lump in my throat suddenly came up. The incredible stress, pain, and fear of the entire experience had suddenly erupted in me. I struggled because I didn't want to cry. The cool, unemotional being was now radiating an overwhelming sense of compassion and love. I looked away and wanted to be strong enough that I could finish what I wanted to say. I just couldn't. I burst into tears as we embraced each other, and I sobbed uncontrollably as she whispered, "It's okay to cry . . . the strong ones cry."

It took some time to compose myself, and I do recall that we spoke but I have no recollection of what specifically we spoke about. I've never been allowed to remember what that discussion was, but I do remember that we talked at length. When it came time for me to leave the ship, there was a strong feeling that we were best of friends. The one female being (she looked like all the others but had a feminine aura about her) was very close to me, as if we had an intimate connection. As I embraced her in front of my car with the other friendly beings around us, she sorrowfully said, "I wish I could stand beside you . . . to face the things you're going to have to face."

Pulling back, I looked into those incredible blue eyes and said, "No . . . that's okay. I understand." As wonderful as these feelings of friendship and camaraderie were, I had to leave. I had important things to do, and this wasn't where I belonged. The same beings that I had been so angry with earlier were now touching me with complex and intense feelings of joy and sadness. It was a remarkable moment between us, and maybe between our species.

So I was taken on board this craft, and I was returned. I don't really know the exact amount of time that transpired from the time I was taken on board, because I don't have all my memories intact. It was probably about an hour to an hour and a half, somewhere in that neighborhood. And when I returned, the transport truck was still there behind my vehicle. I stepped out of the car, glancing into the darkness of the starlit sky; walked into the bathroom at the truck stop; and put some water on my face. I contemplated what, if anything, I should say to anyone. I didn't want to sound like I was crazy. Leaving the washroom, I walked toward the pretty waitress behind the counter. I asked her if she had seen anything. I glanced out the front window. She said, "No dear . . . Are you looking for someone?"

I said, "No, that's okay. They probably already left." Then she asked me if I wanted a cup of coffee. I thought, "I'm not going to be able to get any sleep here, no matter how tired I am." I wanted to get back in my car and get the hell out of there! I ordered a coffee to go.

My sense of what happened that night is that this was a very carefully planned encounter, but just one small step in a much larger plan for an "intervention" in human development. I have a strong belief that the ETs sense a gross spiritual imbalance in us that threatens our survival. Our warlike behavior and destructive technology has exceeded our spiritual development, and we will be facing a tremendous crisis in our near future. The ETs have decided to intervene to help ensure humanity is going to find its way through this dark period. That's the best I can describe it. So their intent is to really play a very subtle role in the background, but they're still going to have to play a role. I don't completely understand it, to be honest with you. Although they are apparently seeking relationships with some individuals, they are very cautious about how this is done. I think, ultimately, their desire is not for us to have a relationship with them but actually to have a better relationship with each other (other human beings). That's their ultimate purpose. And that's another reason why they're trying to be quite subtle about it and trying to remain in the background.

To help share my understanding of this difficult, complex, and emerging phenomenon, I have put a Web site together and written a book. Even after all these years, I still find it difficult to talk about, but realize that people need to know. With so much misinformation out there, I believe we need to educate everyone about what is really happening and encourage more serious scientific investigation. There is one commonality between my current job and what I believe has to happen in the UFO phenomeon. I do a lot of education in the health and safety field. I've seen the benefits of really good educational programs. And I think that we need to do that in the UFO field, because there's certainly a lack of good information out there right now. It's no longer a question of when humanity will contact and interact with extraterrestrials, but rather the much more difficult question of how they have decided to interact with us.

—Jim Moroney
www.aufosg.com

PART 2

Messages and Assistance from the Spirit World

A ghostly warning coming over the CB radio. A timely text message from a trucker's father—who died years earlier in a roll-over accident. One of the most common ways people encounter the spirit world is when a family member or friend on the other side shows up to deliver a message or offer assistance. Is it possible that each industry, like trucking, has its own guardians and ghosts? Or that protective spirits look out for certain travelers on the nation's roadways? From a trusted rig that seems to have a mind of its own when there's danger ahead, to seemingly human helpers in the most unlikely of places, these amazing stories show that, maybe, we are never truly alone.

DECEPTION PASS

I have never been very good at writing, so I ask you to remember that as you read my story of what happened on my trip to the naval air station (NAS) on Whidbey Island off the coast of Washington State and the return to Byron, California.

I was driving for Diablo Trucking out of Byron. They hauled for the government, mainly explosives and freight for the naval air stations and navy bases in the western states. I received the dispatch call about 6:00 A.M. I was up having coffee as usual, as my brain wakes me up about 4:00 A.M. every day. It was about two weeks before Christmas. The next day, I would be taking a load of pilots' personal and launch gear from an aircraft carrier at Alameda station in Oakland to the naval air station on Whidbey Island. The navy flies all the pilots back to the base and the pilots' gear is shipped back by truck.

I packed for a week (you never know what will happen in winter), loaded my clothes and my food into my tractor, and drove to Alameda. I was escorted to the aircraft carrier. I backed up to the conveyor belt, and they loaded my trailer. I never realized what it takes for these pilots to get into the air. I have to say, they really know how to get the job done—they were fast. Now, with my truck loaded and my trailer sealed, I received my manifest. One of the pilots told me that the sooner they got all the gear stored at the NAS, the sooner they would be able to go home for Christmas. I told him I also had a deadline given to me by dispatch, so I would arrive as soon as my log book and weather conditions would allow.

I hadn't even gotten to Dunsmuir, California, and had to chain up. I'm thinking this was going to be a long trip—this was only the second time I ever had to chain up so far down the hill—but the snow was really coming down. I almost fell down when I got out of the cab of the truck. I grabbed the rolls of carpet I use when chaining on ice, praying that Ashland wasn't going to close. That could park me until nine or ten the next morning. Just as I finished up with the bungee cords, the snowplow/sander passed on the way up the mountain. I looked up and said, "thank you."

Back in the cab with the heater on full force trying to thaw out my hands (never could chain with gloves on), I heard from southbound truckers on the CB that chains were coming off at Weed, California. And no chain restrictions on Ashland; storm was staying south of Oregon. Couldn't believe my ears, wow, this was good news, hoping nothing changed (smiled as I turned up the volume on my radio, sang along with my oldies-but-goodies tapes).

I finally reached Weed, pulled my chains and stowed them on the rack, with a prayer I wouldn't have to use them again. I was worried I wouldn't make my deadline to be back in four days through 1,800 miles of unknown weather. I couldn't stop thinking how crazy this was.

I stopped at Fat Harvey's truck stop in Canyonville, Oregon. The café had the worst coffee in at least thirty-five states that I know of (they used metal coffee pots). Funny thing is, the fuel stop next door had pretty good coffee. After my eight hours in the sleeper, I filled my thermos with coffee at the fuel stop, grabbed some powdered mini-donuts, and headed for Whidbey Island.

The only thing I hate more than ice and snow is fog, and it was foggy. Somewhere between Roseburg and Cottage Grove, Oregon (I can't remember, as it was so many years ago), I came to the top of an easy incline and saw three flashing amber lights on my left and three blue on my right at the crest of the hill. It looked like the lights were sitting on top of the asphalt. Totally confused, I slowed way down. When I got to the top, I could see taillights of cars and trucks at the bottom of the grade everywhere, most of them were in the median of the road. A container truck was lying on its left side. I could see Christmas packages in the rear window of one car. I got on the CB and tried to warn anyone in the area to slow down. I geared down and moved slowly past the wrecked vehicles. The road was so icy I thought about stopping, but decided I would end up in the middle of it if I did.

I was going to report the accident, but as I continued on the state police showed up, followed by fire trucks. I had that tingling feeling all over, and then I remembered the lights at the crest of the hill. What was that, a reflection? The emergency vehicles hadn't arrived yet. No, all I could see after I got to the top was red taillights and headlights from the cars and trucks, no amber or blue lights anywhere. I tried to forget the lights but couldn't.

I was almost to Portland and stopped, made myself something to eat, and caught up my logbook before I headed into Washington State. About five hours later, I was on Deception Pass, heading into the NAS. I was taken back—I had never seen anything like it, with the tall redwoods, sandy beach, and blue ocean with the sun shining down. I just wanted to stop and enjoy how beautiful this really was.

Then the bridge came into sight. I needed the whole road to make the turn onto the bridge—not much traffic and I could see everything, so I continued and made the turn onto the bridge. I stopped at the gate and was escorted to the tarmac, where I was told to drive very slowly forward so they could pick all the rocks out of my tires. I backed up to the warehouse dock near the hanger, and they unloaded the trailer. One of the pilots asked me if I was heading right back. I told him I was out of hours and would be staying at the truck stop, if I could find a place to park as it was pretty small. He told me that they were all going to town for dinner and they wanted me to go with them. (I think this forty-nine-year-old trucker-ett surprised the guys in the sky.) They were getting to go home six days early for Christmas because I got their gear delivered two days early.

I have to say I was starved, and ready for something better than a salami sandwich stacked with Ruffles potato chips and sliced dill pickle. I have to confess, in my trucking career I think this was what I survived on, and I never seemed to get tired of this sandwich. Just writing about it makes me want one.

I got to the truck stop, showered, and changed for dinner; they took me to a really nice steak house, really good food and better company. I had a wonderful time with these very special men, who tear through the skies and risk their lives. They energized me. My cheeks hurt from laughing and smiling. It's one of my most remembered times of my trucking career.

After dinner, I was ready for some sleep. I couldn't stop thinking about the amber and blue lights; they kept sneaking into my thoughts. I decided to think about it the next day. I had to turn on the radio to get to sleep, and, believe me, I was exhausted.

Morning came way too fast, and I couldn't seem to get awake. I got up and bought some powdered mini-donuts and coffee and pretripped my truck and trailer. I had enough fuel to get to Fat Harvey's in Canyonville. I wanted to wait as long as possible to fuel up in case there was ice and snow. I needed the weight to climb Ashland.

I started my truck up and tuned my radio to weather-band station to see what the day would bring. Didn't sound bad: some scattered showers in Oregon, no storm warnings.

Well, everything went well until just before Rice Hill, Oregon. Stopped to do a safety check and had a flat tire on inside duel on my tractor. At least I didn't have to go far to get it repaired. I was lucky—no one else was in the tire shop. I couldn't believe it; an hour later, I was back on the road. It was getting dark and the clouds were coming in fast. I needed to get going. I wanted to stay at Fat Harvey's since it was the best place to stay overnight. As I drove, it was so black out you couldn't see much more than the road. A May truck driver passed me, and I could see from his fog lights we were on black ice, no tracks or spray coming from his tires on the road. I slowed down and engaged my interlock. I called him on the CB and let him know; he slowed down, and we traveled together for about forty miles. He said he was going to pull off and get some sleep; I needed to make it to Fat Harvey's, so I kept driving. He called me on the CB to let me know his truck had slid right through the stop sign. I know that feeling; lucky for him there was no traffic. Nothing like driving an unloaded rig on a frozen road—you always want to be eighty thousand pounds in the winter and haul aluminum cans in the summer.

It wasn't much farther when a black and silver cab over tractor and trailer came roaring past me. I'm thinking, who is this stupid driver? My stomach was on the floor. I got on the CB and told him he was driving on ice. No answer. He was about a truck and a half in front of me in the hammer lane when he turned on his emergency flashers. Then his left turn signal came on, and then his brake lights. What the hell is he doing; this guy is going to kill both of us! I let off of the accelerator and slowed down.

I couldn't believe my eyes when I came around a bend on a downgrade. Because of the lights from the black truck I could see the rear end of a trailer with no lights on, three quarters of the way out in the slow lane. I said thank you, God, for my time on earth. I moved my truck over to the hammer lane as fast as I could without wrecking. I couldn't use the brakes; I would jackknife. I was so close to hitting that rig I have no idea how I missed it. Now my stomach was in the sleeper, the hair is standing up on my arms, my knees are like rubber, I'm shaking. A cold chill ran through my body. I wasn't sure I could drive—man that was so crazy. After I took a deep breath and got myself back together so to speak, I realized the black and silver truck was gone.

I wanted to thank this driver for saving my life, but there were no taillights on the road in front of me anywhere. There's no way that truck could have gotten out of my sight that fast—we are talking seconds here. Then I realized I was where the accident had happened at the bottom of the grade on my trip northbound. Now I'm thinking about the amber and blue lights I had seen at the top of the grade. I had no idea what had just happened. I realized that I had never seen any headlights from that black and silver truck and trailer before it was right beside me, which was impossible. It was pitch dark out, I would have seen his lights coming behind me in my mirrors. I pulled over, grabbed my flashlight, and checked to make sure I hadn't hit the trailer in the slow lane. I needed to get out of the truck for a few minutes. I could hardly walk and not just because of the ice on the road. Not a mark on my rig. I really thought it was my time.

I got back in the cab and put her in gear. I heard every sound as I shifted through the gears. I have to say my brain was working overtime. I love what I do, is all I could think of, I was so very thankful I would be able to keep doing it.

I was never so happy to see Fat Harvey's. I parked my truck and went into the café. I ordered coffee, cherry pie à la mode, and called my husband—if I couldn't sleep, why should he? I had to talk to someone.

I got up the next morning, pretripped my truck and fueled her up, checked the weather-band radio, and headed to Byron,

California. I pulled into the yard in Byron, backed into a parking spot, and climbed into the sleeper. I was so tired I couldn't think of driving home. I had made my deadline.

I will never forget my trip to the NAS at Whidbey Island, ever.

—Shirley Andresen

BLUE-EYED MESSENGER
AND DONNER PASS

I n the autumn of 1996, my father passed away. He had been caught cheating on my mother a few times. The first time had got him kicked out of the house, and the second really wasn't a surprise to us at all.

He had gone to visit a friend on the other side of town, when, upon crossing his friend's threshold, he keeled over and died of a massive heart attack. Needless to say, I was called by the police and asked to come back to my mother's house, and I did. I made all the necessary phone calls, and, by the end of the evening, the house was full of family. I was running low on cigarettes, and, knowing my mother was with family, I went to the local gas station to get a few more packs.

As I pulled into the gas station, I had the feeling that my dad's soul just wasn't where it should be. (Don't ask me why; I just felt that way.) As I exited my car, a bum approached me and asked if he could wash my windshield for a little change. I pulled out a five-dollar bill and instead asked him if he would pray for my father who had just passed away. I gave him the money and he went to praying loudly (I might add, it kind of embarrassed me). I looked upon his face, and I felt great relief that all was as it should be. I looked into the bum's eyes, and they were a color so piercing blue, they could stop you in your tracks. I thanked him and asked him his name. He answered, "I'm Irish." Still dumbfounded, I bought my cigarettes and went back home.

Months passed, and every time I passed or went into that gas station I looked for him. A few years later I found him, and asked if he remembered me, and if his name was Irish. He said he didn't remember me, but, yes, his name was Irish. The thing that sent chills down my spine is this: his eyes were almost blackish brown, not the blue I saw so clearly that mournful evening.

I had been driving for almost a year as a commercial driver. Being from California, I hadn't had much experience in snow and ice, but six months earlier I was teaming with a classmate I went to truck-driving school with, and he had jackknifed us in a blizzard three miles outside of Oakley, Kansas. So, needless to say, I learned how to respect the winter conditions real fast. I was getting pretty good at driving the I-80 in all types of weather.

Well it was close to Christmas, and my mother had finally accepted my father's passing, to the point that she could smile again. I was doing short hops from Chicago to California and was totally exhausted, trying to make it home for Christmas. I pulled into the Alamo truck stop and stopped for a break. It was December 23.

I was contemplating getting a little sleep before going over Donner Pass, but I knew that if I did, I might not wake up for a while. I figured I would let fate dictate my next move, as a storm was approaching the summit. I stepped out of the truck to use the restroom and was walking behind a few other drivers. I was about ten feet behind them when one of the drivers turned around and told me, "If you're trying to get home, you better go over the pass right now!"

I looked at him because I didn't know him and had never talked to him. Then I saw those same blue eyes I had seen the night my father passed away. I didn't hesitate. I turned around, jumped in my truck, and headed up Donner Pass. As I went up the mountain, I turned the squelch on my CB all the way up, so as to hear any new road conditions etcetera. I reached the second rest area (as you're heading west) and stopped to use the restroom there. As I left that rest area, I heard on the CB that they had shut the pass down behind me, and the snow was falling pretty good. Had I not heeded that driver's words, I would have been stuck there during Christmas, as it stayed closed for a day and a half. I made it back to Los Angeles after dropping my load in Frisco, and my mother had a smile for the first time on Christmas since my father had passed away the Christmas before.

To this day, if I see piercing blue eyes like that, I listen to the words being spoken. I have never seen those eyes again—but I'm always looking.

—Mark L.

"FLORILLI, STOP"

Here is my story: I was driving in a blinding snowstorm on I–70 across Colorado at night; I was running team at the time and I drove nights. Well, approaching Glenwood Springs, Colorado, I had not seen another truck or anything in about twenty minutes or so going east. All of a sudden, clear as day out of my CB, I hear, "Florilli, stop." (Florilli was the name of the company I was driving for at the time.) I did stop twenty feet from a boulder that had fallen in the road. Here is where it gets weird: there was no one behind me or that had come the other way.

—Harold E. Benton

GHOSTLY HAND IN ALABAMA

The experience I had happened in early 2000. I was team driving and we drove a five and five. I had been driving for about three hours in my five-hour drive. It was around four o'clock in the morning, and most drivers know that four to six in the morning is a hard time to drive—you start getting sleepy.

So, about 4:00 A.M., I was driving along, and I start getting sleepy. My team partner was in the back; the curtain was pulled, so he could get his break in. I know I was getting sleepy; my eyes were getting heavy, and my head was nodding. Thank goodness there was not much traffic on the road. I was in Alabama when this happened. I'm driving along, and my eyes keep closing and opening, closing and opening, and I'm doing everything that I can think of—rolling the window down to get fresh air, kind of patting my face, opening my eyes, you know, anything I could think of that would keep me going for a little while. But I know I must have just totally relaxed and went to sleep. And all of sudden, I just felt someone grab my arm between my elbow and my shoulder, just a firm grab on it, and it totally woke me up.

And I glanced back—I was already weaving across the road—and I glanced back at the curtain. I thought maybe it was my partner that was getting up. You know when the truck was weaving, it was a little unsteady, and I thought maybe it was my partner that had grabbed my arm. But no, the curtain was still closed. I drove on for just a few more minutes, I was getting too sleepy, and I decided I just couldn't drive anymore. If I continued, you know, there's a possibility that I would have wrecked the truck.

So I know I had a guardian angel looking out for me that night. Because I felt a definite pressure on my arm that woke me up. My father was a truck driver. He died in the late eighties, in 1989, and about ten years later, I started truck driving. And I guess I feel he is out here, kinda looking out for me, you know?

—Dellcina Holcomb

TEXT MESSAGE

I was driving into Texas from Oklahoma, on U.S. 52, I think, but not sure of that. My father was an OTR driver who died in 2000 in a rollover when a load of scrap iron shifted. Anyway, I was pushing hard and fighting to stay up. I had woken up multiple times to rumble strips, but decided to push on no matter what. But as I completed a pass and was merging back to my right, my father was sitting in the seat beside me. He told me there was a rest area just across the Texas border. I said, "It would be full and I couldn't stop, anyway."

He said, "Well then, I'll stop you."

I awoke four hours later at a rest area just across the Texas border, parked perfectly. An unknown text on my phone read, "No load is worth your life. Love Dad."

I swear this to be true.

—Jim Bradshaw

UNINVITED PASSENGER

Growing up, I had always heard stories that my uncle Jim had some unexplainable occurrences happen to him while being out on the road as a truck driver. Recently, I became curious about the subject and decided to ask him about these experiences. I knew that he was a no-nonsense kind of guy, and whatever he told me would absolutely be the truth.

Jim relayed to me that one day, in the summer of 1985, while at a stop in Michigan, he saw a special sale on bottles of Coca-Cola, three for a dollar. So he purchased three, and, when he got back inside the cab of the truck, he tucked two within easy reach up under the mattress on the bed behind him and opened one up to drink immediately. About two hours later, he became thirsty again, and reached back to feel around for a second bottle. Coming up empty-handed, he was surprised and frustrated enough to pull over and look for the missing sodas. He removed the mattress and completely searched the entire cab, but the two extra bottles of Coca-Cola were nowhere to be found! They had simply vanished.

Then, shockingly, approximately two weeks later they turned back up. They were exactly where he had put them, underneath the mattress, and ice-cold, too! It was a hot summer day, and that space was not air-conditioned. Even the air-conditioning in the truck itself hardly ever worked. Yet here he found these two ice-cold bottles of Coca-Cola precisely as he had left them two weeks prior. Family members speculated as to how this could be. Jim's brother-in-law Randy* had recently passed, and some wondered if Randy had something to do with it. Randy did take trips with Jim sometimes. He definitely loved an ice-cold Coca-Cola. Jim had inherited a briefcase of Randy's that he kept in the truck with him. Could Randy's spirit be hanging out with Jim, playing tricks on him?

Then, in 2003, Jim had a ghostly encounter that really shook him up. He had stopped at a CT terminal in Birmingham, Alabama, to get some rest before getting back out on the road. He had fallen asleep but awoke due to a cold chill that had taken over the cab, despite him being tucked under covers. He was sleeping facing the back of the truck, and, when he awoke, he looked to his left. The curtains were somewhat open, and through them he saw a little girl sitting at the edge of his bed. She was on her knees with her elbows on the side of the bed and her face in her hands, just staring at him with a big smile on her face. She looked to be about five to six years old, with long dark hair. He jumped up out of the bed and said aloud, "Where the heck did you come from?" He thought he was speaking to a real child who had somehow got inside his truck . . . until she just faded before his eyes!

I was amazed by this story and asked Jim if he knew who this girl could be. He said he didn't, and in describing her he said she looked just like a picture he had seen of his wife, Kyra, when she was a little girl. I found this detail to be quite intriguing, since I knew Kyra actually had a sister who had passed away as an infant of just six hours old, due to a ruptured appendix. I wondered if this could be the spirit of Kaelie Sue just materializing as a young child rather than as an infant.

Since that time, Jim believes this little girl has followed him, playing jokes and moving things around in the truck as well as when he is home. Years later, when a friend with mediumistic abilities told him he had a little-girl spirit around him who liked to play pranks, he was not surprised at all, since he had in fact seen her himself. The friend told Jim to say out loud, "Okay, ha, ha, the joke is over, put it back now," and whatever was missing would soon appear. Jim now says this aloud every time something goes missing, and, within a day or two, sure enough, it will appear back where it was supposed to be.

I wondered if the missing Coke bottles weren't also this little girl, even though that experience was eighteen years earlier. Could one occurrence be Randy and the other Kaelie Sue, the two siblings of his wife that had prematurely passed? And if so, why did they come to Jim rather than to their sister, Kyra? Is it because a trucker is easier to connect to, spending so much time on the road alone? I asked Jim if he had ever had any experiences like this as a child or before he started driving. He said he had not. These strange occurrences only started after he became a trucker.

—Stacy Eldridge

*Some names have been changed to protect privacy.

THE MAN IN THE RAIN

I am always interviewing flight attendants and pilots for my podcast, *Betty in the Sky with a Suitcase*. I did an episode called "Airline X-files" about haunted airplanes and the like. My favorite story was from this very senior flight attendant. She is sort of old-fashioned and proper. She said that, years ago, before cell phones, her car broke down on a California highway. It was nighttime and pouring down rain. Having heard horror stories of what can happen to single women on the side of the road, she was hesitant to get out of her car and walk to the call box.

At that moment a car stopped and a really good-looking man got out. He walked to her car and tapped on the window. She rolled down the window, and he said "Do you want me to walk you to the call box?" and she replied "Oh, yes!"

He escorted her to the call box, and she called Triple A. The man walked her to her car and said, "Would you like me to wait with you till the tow truck gets here?" She said yes and got back in her car. The man stood outside till the tow truck got there and then got back in his car and drove off.

For days, she kept thinking about that nice-looking, kind gentleman who had helped her. Something was nagging her about him. Then two days later, she sat straight up in her bed in the middle of the night and realized—*he wasn't wet.*

—Betty Thesky
Author of the book *Betty in the Sky with a Suitcase*
http://betty.libsyn.com

MICHELIN TIRE MAN ON I-94

In March of 1985, I was returning to Minnesota from my Grandma Morgan's funeral in Marmarth, North Dakota, a small town near the North Dakota–Montana border. My sister Betsy and my brothers Randall and Sam and I were going home a day earlier than the rest of our family because the three of them had already missed a couple of days of school and couldn't take any more time off. (Betsy and Randall were in college and Sam was in junior high.) And I was anxious to get back home to my kids, who were seven and five, and my husband. At twenty-three, I was the oldest in the group—I mention this because if we'd been a little older, or wiser, or had any money at all, we might have pulled off the road before things got so strange.

We left Marmarth around 1:00 P.M., right after lunch at the church. The first part of the trip home was completely normal. As we drove, we reminisced about our Grandma and Grandpa Morgan and visiting our cowboy cousins each summer when we were growing up. We speculated that we wouldn't be getting back to North Dakota very often now that both our Grandma and Grandpa Morgan were gone. It added to the sense of loss we already felt.

I drove for the first four hours or so. We started out on Highway 12, a mostly deserted two-lane that runs east-west from Marmarth through the small town of Rhame, then Bowman. At Bowman, we turned north on Highway 85, which meets the interstate (I–94) near Dickinson.

When we got to Bismarck, we switched drivers and Randall took a turn driving. It was just starting to snow when he got behind the wheel. Our family trips to North Dakota had always taken place in the summertime—we kids had never experienced the deadly winter weather that could come howling across the plains out of nowhere. The snow quickly became a swirling, blinding whiteout that never let up for the next twelve hours. Conversation in the car ceased as we realized how dangerous the driving conditions were. The blizzard was so bad that the only other vehicles we saw on the freeway were a few semi-trucks and, weirdly, a couple of school buses. Solemn-faced kids looked out at us from the bus windows as it passed our car, and the sight of kid-filled yellow school buses out in the treacherous night was surreal and disturbing. I tried to get some sleep while Randall drove, but I was so anxiety-ridden by the thought of us crashing that I barely even dozed off.

We really should have pulled off the freeway, like nearly every other vehicle on the road had done. But none of us had any cash or credit cards. We could have spent the night sitting in a hotel lobby or at an all-night truck stop, but for some reason that idea never occurred to us. Besides, it was so difficult to even see the road that we were afraid of ending up in the ditch if we tried to get off the highway. So we kept going, following semi-truck taillights whenever we could.

For the next couple hundred miles, we drove in a hypnotic tunnel of swirling snow. The never-changing visual scenario, coupled with the acute stress of the drive, made time feel warped and weird. It felt like we were trapped in a world from which there was no escape, an endless vertical sinkhole of twirling snow. After nearly eight hours of driving in these conditions, Randall was exhausted. But he somehow powered through until we got to his school, St. John's University, which is about sixty miles north of the Twin Cities. It seems crazy to me now that we didn't all pile into his dorm room till morning came (even though St. John's was a Catholic college for men only). But we didn't. It was like sleep deprivation and relentless stress had reduced my reasoning ability to a single desperate goal: get home.

After we dropped Randall off, I drove for the last leg of the journey. At this point, we had been on the road for around fourteen hours. We had lost an hour (due to the time change), so it was a little after 4:00 A.M., but I knew we were almost home. I braced myself for another few hours of driving in the mesmerizing, kaleidoscopic snow. When I saw the red taillights of a semi ahead of us, I locked onto them, desperate for a beacon in the storm.

I noticed something hanging off the back of the truck that, at first, looked like white rags or a raggedy tarp flapping in the wind. I watched it closely, thinking about what I would do if it came loose and flew off. As I continued to stare, I realized that what I had thought were rags now actually looked like something standing on the back of the truck, clamped onto the vertical pipe on the truck door with what looked like pincers or a handcuff. The thing on the back of the truck resembled the Michelin Tire Man. I kept looking at it, trying to focus so I could figure out what I was really seeing. With a jolt that made me feel hot and almost sick to my stomach, I realized I could see a cartoonish face. Whatever the thing was, it seemed to be looking at me and waving, like "c'mon, c'mon!" I kept looking at it, and I kept seeing it. The tire man seemed animated, like he would look ahead and then back at us to see if we were still following.

I was certain I was hallucinating. I knew I shouldn't be driving. I knew I should try to pull over at the next exit, no matter how invisible the exit ramps were. But I couldn't take my eyes off the Michelin Tire Man on the back of the truck. I was really hoping he would disappear. The fact that he didn't was freaking me out.

Suddenly Betsy, who had been dozing off beside me in the passenger seat, said, "Do you see the marshmallow man on the back of the truck?"

"You can see it, too?" I was shocked. It was bad enough that I could see it. How was it possible that Betsy and I both saw the same completely freakish thing? My brother Sam was asleep in the backseat, but we didn't wake him up.

I said, "He's got rings, like the Michelin Tire Man." Betsy said she could see the rings, too. She could also see his face, and see him waving us forward. We watched the Michelin Tire Man for nearly two hours, only losing sight of him as the semi he was riding on occasionally disappeared from view. A few minutes later, the truck's red taillights would come into view again, and

the tire man was still there. Some part of my mind was thinking, "This cannot be happening." I knew it was bizarre, even for
a hallucination, that Betsy and I both saw what looked like a
cartoon character (instead of, say, a guardian or guide). But another part of me was so relieved to feel like someone was looking
out for us that I didn't care what it was.

We lost sight of the semi-truck with the Michelin Man just
before we got to Minneapolis. By then it was starting to get light
out and the snow seemed to be tapering off. I had been hoping
that when the morning came, we could get a good look at the
Michelin Man. I wanted to see if he was real or at least something
more than a bunch of rags, but we never saw the semi-truck again.
I was disappointed, but, truthfully, at that moment, I was thinking more about being back in familiar territory, about the sun
coming up, about all of us being safe. I said a prayer of thanks as
we passed the familiar downtown Minneapolis exits. I dropped
Betsy off at the College of St. Thomas in St. Paul and headed for
home with my little brother. As the tension started to leave my
body, it was replaced by a debilitating exhaustion that felt like
lead, and I struggled to stay awake for the last twenty miles of
the trip. When we got to my house, as I walked up the sidewalk
with Sam, all I kept thinking was, "We're alive" and "I get to see
my kids again."

The Michelin Man encounter was so outlandishly weird that
for many years, I hardly told anyone about it. I figured it had
been some sort of prolonged hallucination brought on by exhaustion and stress and being trapped in a never-ending sideways
snow tunnel for twelve hours. After all, what symbolizes road

safety more aptly than the friendly Michelin Tire Man? Although, it *was* pretty strange that Betsy and I hallucinated the exact same thing . . .

More than a decade after our experience with the Michelin Man, I came across an article in the U.K.'s hipster paranormal magazine *Fortean Times* titled "Claw Men from Outer Space." The article described an unusual UFO contact experience in Florida in which the article referred to the aliens as Claw Men, but the illustration bore a striking resemblance to the Michelin Tire Man. I showed Betsy the article and she, too, thought that the aliens in the illustration looked like what we had seen. I did some research online and discovered that, although rare, there have been at least three recorded encounters with a being that looks like the Michelin Tire Man. According to what I've been able to find, the first encounter with a Michelin Tire Man (actually two men) occurred in Spain in 1960. Another sighting happened in the U.K. in 1962 or 1963, and a third took place in Kansas in 1976.

So was the Michelin Tire Man actually some sort of extraterrestrial or astral being? I've read everything I can find, and I still don't know the answer. It makes no sense to me that an alien would ride on the back of a semi-truck during a blizzard to help some scared kids make it home safely. But it seems equally unlikely that a guardian spirit would appear to two scared young travelers as a tire-company cartoon mascot. So I find myself in the same predicament as the proverbial Irish old-timer, who, when asked if he believed in leprechauns, said, "No—but they're real." Even though I can't explain it, I know what we saw.

—Annie Wilder

'65 MUSTANG ON CALIFORNIA'S I–10

This happened in 2003 when my mom, my little sister, and I were traveling from Arizona to California to visit my older brother, who was living just outside of San José at the time. On the way to visit my brother, we were driving on a four-lane highway, the I–10, heading east. My little sister was asleep in the backseat, my mom was driving, and I was in the passenger seat.

As we drove, we were following this '65 or '66 brown Ford Mustang that was barely able to do the speed limit of 75 mph. We stayed behind the Mustang. As we drove, we went into the left lane to pass a semi-truck. To give you a little bit of a visual, we were at about the middle of the truck's trailer, right in his blind spot, and the Mustang was right behind the cab of the semi. The semi decided it wanted to switch lanes and started coming into the lane that we were currently in. With the semi switching lanes, we were being forced into the ditch to our left with not enough time to slow down to avoid it. At this point the semi saw the Mustang, and went back into his own lane.

About ten minutes after avoiding what would have been a tragic accident, my mom and I noticed the Mustang had disappeared into thin air. There was literally nowhere for it to go. We didn't have an exit for miles—we were in the middle of nowhere. Now, mind you, this Mustang was as solid as you or I. I know people may think, oh you probably passed it, but we didn't. It was in front of us the whole time—until it vanished.

—Reggie Growth

MESSAGE FROM THE CEMETERY

I'm a small-town undertaker; part of my job is selling tombstones and the pictures and vases that go with them.

A trucker, a colorful, well-liked swashbuckler named Manuel Hernandez,* died after a long, long bout with a serious heart condition, and I directed his huge funeral.

In defiance and denial, Manuel smoked and drank and partied to the last. Minutes after he passed away at our little hospital, thirty feet from Manuel's room, Manuel's first grandchild, named Manuel, of course, came screaming into the world.

Manuel's son and daughter-in-law lived in the same large farmhouse as Manuel. The night after the couple and their baby came home from the hospital, Manuel's daughter-in-law was nursing little Manuel, and the phone by the bed in old Manuel's room rang. The new mom went in and answered it, and a rather indistinct male voice said, "Congratulations, Honey, and thank you." The line then went dead. The next morning, she went into the empty bedroom to get something, and she remembered she had needed the cord from Manuel's phone in another room and had disconnected it several weeks before. She checked—the phone was still disconnected.

Months later, Manuel's wife, Maribelle, came to my office to order a tombstone. I sold her a double-wide granite stone, and she insisted that a picture of a Hernandez Trucking Peterbilt be engraved on Manuel's side of the stone. She ordered a large white marble vase to be placed on the granite base of the stone.

When the stone arrived from the quarry, I set it in the cemetery and cemented the vase onto the base. I called Maribelle and told her to go out to the cemetery to take a look at it. Twenty minutes later she called me from her home and said that the stone was "just beautiful" and she wanted to know how I had managed to find a vase the same deep turquoise color as Manuel's trucks. I told her that the vase was white when I set it. I asked her to meet me at the cemetery. When we got there, the vase, indeed, was bright white; then, as we watched, it turned a deep turquoise color. After a few minutes, it turned white again.

Always a skeptic, I called the marble dealer and asked him if any possible chemical reaction, maybe caused by something in the cemetery water, could cause the color change. The dealer had never, ever had a white marble vase change color, nor had he ever heard of such a thing happening. He said the marble was impervious. Over the next several days, many other people saw the vase change, but the phenomenon stopped after a couple of weeks.

Several months later, on a warm Sunday morning in April, Maribelle called. She said "You've got to see this. Come out to the cemetery." When I arrived, Maribelle was looking at the vase, which was a distinct dusky-rose color. I asked her if the color meant anything to her. She told me that "dusky rose" was the shade of her wedding gown and that it was their fortieth anniversary that day.

I fully expect to hear more from Manuel. When he was alive, he never hesitated to speak his mind, and, obviously, not much has changed . . .

—Joel Whitehurst

*Names have been changed to protect privacy.

LAST GOOD-BYE

We were holding a funeral for a lifelong truck driver, an Irish Okie who was known for his kind heart, his perpetual grin, and his love for a good practical joke. I was directing the service.

As the minister finished his sermon, I was in the back of the chapel, preparing to walk to the front of the chapel and dismiss the large crowd of mourners. Pastor Berry ended his talk with his customary blessing, and I started up the aisle.

A third of the way to the front, I heard the distinctive sound of a diesel engine starting and running, and I paused. I noticed that a large model truck, attached to a floral piece next to the casket, was making the sound. The headlights on the truck went off and on, and the truck model blew a very realistic and very loud air horn several times. I remember thinking that the diesel had provided quite a fitting ending for the service.

I showed the guests out of the main chapel and then went into the family room to show the family past the casket for their final good-byes. I mentioned to the son of the deceased that the truck was a nice touch, and asked him if it was radio-controlled. "We thought you did that," he said. "We were going to thank you."

I checked it out, and the truck was not radio-controlled. There are little buttons on it to activate the start-up, the lights, and the horn. The florist had bought it at a toy store when the family requested a diesel floral piece . . .

There was nobody within twelve feet of that truck when the incident occurred. A hundred and fifty people witnessed it, but didn't know what they had seen . . .

—Joel Whitehurst

TRUNK TROUBLE

My dad and my grandmom were not close. She gave up custody of him when he was young, and they didn't have a very good relationship until he and my mom had children. We got to see her on holidays and special occasions, and I always enjoyed seeing her—she was wickedly funny. Once I was able to drive I went to visit her often, and she would tell me all the dirty jokes she had heard since I saw her last and all the jokes she would play on her health aides that came to care for her. She was confined to a wheelchair as she had both of her legs amputated, so she couldn't get out and really enjoyed the company. Sadly, when I was nineteen years old, just as she and I were really "enjoying" our relationship, she passed away. My father was working when we got the phone call. He was recovering from a heart attack, and I rushed out of the house to go be with him. As I was pulling out of our driveway, I looked in my rearview mirror and my trunk popped open, which was strange! So I got out and closed it . . .

On my way to Grandmom's home, I stopped at my brother's friend's house to see if my brother was there. I wanted to let him know what had happened and ask him to go home. I knocked.

He wasn't there, so back into the car I went. Pulling out of the driveway, I look in the rearview mirror . . . trunk popped open! So I got out and closed it . . . yank, pull, tug, it wasn't budging. Drove up the block and turned the corner, and my trunk popped open . . . so I pull over and slam it, yank, tug, shake it. It is closed tight . . . so I sat for a few minutes trying to let go of the frustration, and I begin my forty-minute ride to my grandmom's. I pulled out onto the main road, and dang it if the trunk didn't open again . . . by then a feeling came over me and I KNEW it was my grandmom . . . this is definitely her sense of humor. Due to her having her legs amputated she had no knees. So, we called her Nonni ("no-knee"), Italian for "Grandmom." She was a funny lady. So I pulled over, closed the trunk, and said out loud, "Nonni, I know this is you, and I am going to miss you terribly, but this is starting to make me angry. I am trying to get to my dad!" and it stopped and I made my way to meet my dad.

As I pulled onto her road I could see police cars, the ambulance, and my dad's truck. I got out of my car and took a deep breath and went to the front door. As I was walking in the front door a woman grabbed me by the elbow and took me into another room. Confused, I looked at her, and she said she was Grandmom's health aide and had found her this morning passed away. Her hospital bed was in the living room, and she had fallen out of bed trying to reach the phone. I began to cry, and she said, "You are Stacey, right?"

I said, "Yeah."

She began to tell me that they were going to be removing her body and she didn't want me to see it. She said my Nonni talked about me all the time and never tired of telling her our stories and showing her my pictures. She also told me not more than thirty seconds before I walked in the door they had finished picking my Nonni's body off of the floor and covered her. Then it hit me! Nonni was stalling me so I wouldn't be there to see her where she had died on the floor. I told her aide the story, and she threw her arms around me, and we both began to cry.

A few days later, my mom and I went shopping for clothes for her viewing; she told me she was in the store the day before and saw a dress she really thought I would like. It wasn't black, but she just really liked this dress. It was a coral color, very pretty, but I had found a blue pantsuit to wear. The next night we went to Nonni's viewing, and I walked up to her casket to say my good-byes and could not believe my eyes—Nonni was going to be buried in the EXACT dress my mom tried to talk me into buying! I began to cry and laugh, and I knew she was never going to leave me, and I felt her arm around me, laughing.

—Stacey Burdash

STRANGER IN THE WOODS

This was back in 1988. I was traveling to go to college. I had been out of school for a number of years. I was a single dad, and I wanted to go try to get my life rebooted. I went in for my GED, passed that, and then went in for my ACT and had to go to Winona State to take the test.

So I'm on my way there, really trying to make this change, and I have this weird thing happen underneath the hood—all of a sudden steam just starts pouring out of my car, and I'm losing pressure. I know nothing about cars—I'm the worst guy in the world when it comes to this. So I get off on the exit and it's after La Crosse. I mean, I'm heading into . . . there's like the Cascade Ski Resort off of Highway 94, which I'm driving on. So I pull off and I pull up into this little dark, dank, like, roadside rest area.

And again, I know *absolutely nothing*, about cars. So I'm screwed. And I've got this old '69 Plymouth Fury—huge big boat, right? I pop open the hood. And I'm standing there scratching my head like something's gonna jump out at me and tell me what needs to be fixed. When suddenly, just *swoosh* out of the blue, comes this guy walking up, a very hippie-looking fella. He walks up and goes, "Hey, man, what's goin' on?"

And I said, "I don't know. I don't know anything about cars. I'm trying to get to Winona. I gotta take the test early in the morning; I'm taking my ACT. I don't know what I'm gonna do. I don't have any money on me. I don't even know how to get this thing fixed."

And he goes, "Well, let's see what we can figure out." And he goes walking over and there's this car sitting in the parking lot. And he goes and he pops open the trunk and comes back with this little tool kit and a flashlight and he looks underneath the hood. And he goes, "Oh, yeah, you blew out your *flippity-bloppety-bleu*" (which is the technical term I'm using, the "flippity-bloppety-bleu").

And there is a little, like, rubbery cap thing. And he goes, "Hmm. Let me just check something." And he flips open the top of his tool-chest tray, and he has this miniature little bag; and he opens up this bag and there's this little rubber cap thing. And he goes, "Look what I have." And then he just slips it right over the nozzle. Then he says, "Now you're gonna let this car cool down for about a half an hour, and then you're gonna go over and you're gonna fill the radiator with cool water again, and you'll be ready to go."

And I said, "Oh, great, thanks!" I don't . . . I don't have any money to pay you for this." I mean, what are the odds this cat's got the exact little rubber stopper I need for a '69 Plymouth Fury in his car?

And he goes, "No, no, no, don't worry about it. Just do a nice deed for somebody else sometime."

I'm like, "Really? Well, thank you very much." And then I

started to think, *what the hell is this guy doing all alone in a forest-preserve area?* And I got a little creeped out. And he's *barefoot*, which is weird—right? And he just had, like, come out of the woods. Literally, as I was standing there, he just came walking out of the woods barefoot and did this. And then he just *swoosh* goes right back in, and that was it. End of story. Didn't see him again. Didn't hear a word from him. Nothing!

I got my car going, made it to school, and passed my test. But I always thought that was just the weirdest thing—that out of all the places in the world, only one vehicle sitting there, this guy comes out of the woods, helps me fix my car, and then vanishes back into the woods again.

—Dave Schrader

Coauthor of *The Other Side: A Teen's Guide to*

Ghost Hunting and the Paranormal

www.darknessradio.com

MONTANA BLIZZARD GHOST

It was December 31, 1987, New Year's Eve—a frigid and snowy day in the small town of Dillon, Montana. I was an EMT (emergency medical technician) and on call. My boyfriend, Hank, had come into town. Hank was an over-the-road trucker who traveled the road and lived his life by breaking every law there was to be made. I suspected that Hank was using drugs and found out later he was not only using but also selling drugs across the country and into Mexico and Canada.

While Hank and I were having dinner at the local hangout, I got a page for an ambulance and had to go on a run. The paging system sent this message: "fourteen-year-old male having seizures." I rushed to the ambulance building, where I joined my EMT partner, Susan. We jumped into the ambulance and hit the road with the lights flashing and sirens blasting. We came upon the site where the police were surrounding the young man, who appeared to be experiencing grand mal seizures. We grabbed our gear and ran into the situation. The police were asked to help us get him on the board so we could transport. It took six men to hold him down as we strapped him to the board. We sped off to the ER.

When we arrived at the ER the young man seemed to have calmed down a bit. The attending physician cut the tape we had strapped across his head to hold it in place. The young man opened his eyes. If there was a devil, I was looking him in the eye. His blood-ridden eyes were bulging out of their sockets, piercing each one of us. He looked at Susan and started to vomit. It was projectile vomiting, and his head was jerking around as verbal gibberish came from deep within his throat. It was like a scene from the movie *The Exorcist*. Susan was covered with the grayish sticky vomit. I had never seen such a thing in my career.

The doctor quickly restrapped the boy's head to the board and demanded we take him to a hospital one hour away that had services that could help with this situation. We headed north to Butte on the icy, snowy roads of Interstate 15. We arrived in Butte, and the ER physicians quickly diagnosed that the young man had cocaine in his system. The vomit, which continued for some time on the road, appeared to be brain matter and other destroyed tissues. Their impression was that the cocaine was probably laced with some toxic chemicals that literally melted the young man's sinus system and went into his brain and destroyed tissue.

Susan and I cleaned up and headed home. The roads of snow and ice were simple compared to the situation I had just experienced. We got back to Dillon and cleaned up the ambulance; then I went home to try and get some sleep.

I tossed and turned in my bed. I was thinking about Hank. What was he up to? Did he bring this laced cocaine into town? My mind would not stop racing, so I got up and got into my faithful Chevy Cavalier and went driving around. I drove past the nightclub where Hank would hang out, but his truck was not around. I figured he must have gone to party somewhere else. I kept driving. I headed out of town, toward the mountains of Montana that give me some peace of mind.

There wasn't even a trucker out there on the road. By now it was 3:00 A.M. I was near one of my favorite places in the country, Yellowstone Park. I was getting hungry, but the thought of food and visions of vomit just ruined my natural instinct to eat. Furthermore, I had no food with me. I took the cutoff to get to a secluded area and headed into the snowy morning.

The snow was about eight inches deep. My car had front-wheel drive, and I had taken it everywhere and never got stuck, so I felt safe. I traveled for miles when I realized that I was on the wrong road and that, moreover, the snow had gotten about fourteen inches deep and it had started to snow quite heavily. I studied the situation and realized I had better not stop. The snow was too deep and wet. The road, as if there was a road, was disappearing in front of my eyes. Perhaps I was experiencing snow blindness. All I could see was white. I kept on driving.

Hours passed. The snow was so deep on the ground it was coming up over the hood of the car. I was getting concerned, especially when I realized I had no water or food with me. I reached into the jockey box and found a piece of gum. That was all I had. Then I knew I was in trouble. The gas tank was half full, and I calculated that, if I did get stuck, I could keep warm for about six hours. My plan would be turn the engine off until I got too cold, turn the engine on to warm up, and perhaps I could last for a day or so. Then somebody could find me.

Find me! I didn't even know where I was. Somewhere in Yellowstone Park. But where? With the snowfall I estimated that within the next few hours the car with me in it would be buried under a blanket of snow if I were to stop. Then how would anyone find me? I kept on driving.

I knew I was in big trouble now. I thought about my daughter. She was with her dad for the weekend. Would I ever see her again? I was sure my family would be wondering what was up with me; we were supposed to have New Year's Day dinner at my brother's house, and I was never late, unless I was on a call for the ambulance. The snow was getting deeper and now was going over the top of the car as I kept driving. I had no other options. I had to keep going.

Then I knew it was over. I saw in my mind's eye my funeral next spring when they found me and the car. I was done for. I started to sniffle a little bit when the snow broke for a moment. I was able to see something in the distance. It was a grove of trees. Could it be real, or was it a mirage? I turned the wheels toward the trees and saw that they were real aspen trees. I drove toward them. I recognized I was getting into deeper snow, so I turned back to the path that somehow I knew where to drive.

My racing mind created the fantasy that if there were trees, perhaps there would be a ranch close by. And a new problem was emerging. I had to go pee. I knew I couldn't stop. I might get stuck, so I kept on going.

I lost track of time. The snow was giving me a break and the snow on the ground was getting less. I figured I must be coming to lower ground. Then my bladder said NO MORE! I had to stop.

The snow was about ten inches deep. I stopped the car and left the engine running while I got out to go pee. I went to the back of the car, as if I had to hide from someone, and pulled down my pants and started to relieve my bladder.

Ahhhhhhh! Relief! Then I thought I heard a vehicle somewhere close. Shit! I tried to hurry and finish my job, but out of nowhere this blue and white 1960ish Ford pickup pulled up. I quickly pulled up my pants and went to the front of the car. There was a white male with long hair, a beard, and mustache, topped off with a brown cowboy hat, driving the truck.

My mind was going crazy. At that time in the state of Montana, there had been a young female athlete that had been mountain training for a marathon, and two men abducted her to "make her their wife." I knew this guy must be one of those guys. The man stopped his truck, opened the door, and yelled at me. "What the hell are you doing up here?"

"What do you mean?" I meekly responded. He approached me in a bold manner and asked me again, "What the hell are you doing up here? Where did you come from? Where are you going?"

I was so scared. I looked around to see if I could get away from him. I was making the effort to get into my car when he approached me directly and spoke into my face. "Where in the hell did you come from? Who are you?"

Shaking in my boots I pointed to my tracks that went up the mountain. "From there. I came from over there."

He noticed my license plates. "You're from Montana. What are you doing here?"

I replied "Yes, I am from Montana. Where am I? Who are you?"

He was so close to my face I could smell his breath. Chewing tobacco! I could see his teeth were stained from the disgusting habit. He demanded an answer. "I asked who are you? What are you doing?"

I told him who I was and that I guess I had taken the wrong turn back near Yellowstone Park. He shook his head and then called me a liar. "There is no way you came from over there. That mountain road is closed until June. Nobody goes across that road in the winter. It's impossible!"

Bewildered, I leaned against my car door and asked where in the hell I was.

"You're in Idaho. Don't you know any better?" he shouted. Now he was pissing me off. Calling me a liar was the last straw. My thoughts of him taking me as his wilderness wife were overridden by my impatience with a stupid, ignorant man.

I looked him in the eye and said, "I don't give a rat's ass what you think. I came from over there and I have to get home. I'm late for dinner!"

He stepped back and scratched his greasy head under that old cowboy hat. "Well, I guess I better help you get out of here. You're about a hundred miles from Dubois, Idaho. Do you see the outlines of the road out there?" He pointed out into the field. I could barely make it out, but I said I did. "Get in your car and I will follow you. If you start to get off track I will honk my horn.

When I honk you better stop, or you are going to have big trouble to deal with. Now get going! I'll follow you."

I jumped into my car and headed out. He was right on my bumper. This break in the personal confrontation had given me time to think about this man and where I was. Idaho. This state is known as a home for the skinheads. But this guy had hair. Idaho also has many other groups that operate free from the constraints of the government. Maybe he was part of a cult or something. My mind kept racing.

Honk! Honk!!! I looked in the rearview mirror, and he was waving to me to stop. I stopped my car and he came to my door. I knew this was it. He was going to take me right there. Take me to his cult, where who knows what they would do to me?

He pointed to the horizon. "Do you see the telephone poles down there? There's a small town down there. If you knock on the door of the house behind the gas station, they will help you. Now stay on this road. Do you understand?"

"Yes," I said. He stood up real tall and tugged at his belt as he took a big breath. "I will keep following you. Stay on the road!"

He went to his truck and I started to drive. He was right on my bumper. I kept an eye on the road as well as an eye on him.

We must have gone for miles. I could see the town getting closer. I looked into the mirror to check on him and he was gone. Gone! Vanished! I stopped my car and got out to see if I could see where he went. He was nowhere in sight. I jumped back into my car and turned around to see where he had gone. I drove back toward the mountains. Then I noticed there was only one set of tracks in the snow. Mine.

I made it to the town and purchased some gasoline. I headed to Montana in a bewildered state of mind. I was hungry, confused, angry, and scared. When I got to my brother's house, my family was furious. The police had started looking for me. They knew I had been upset about the young man and the cocaine issue and thought I must have gotten myself into some mess. I was known for that!

I never shared this story with anyone for weeks. Then one day Alberta Cassidy asked me out of the blue what had happened to me on that January day. I looked at her and wondered why she would ask me a question like that. Alberta was in her late eighties. She was a metaphysician as well as a noted astrologer. I told her my story. She told me the cowboy was a spirit. A good ghost. An angel.

Maybe she was right. I thought maybe it was the spirit of the young man that was now considered brain-dead. Perhaps he was trying to help me. Maybe it was his spirit that was aiding me in return for my trying to help him.

I continued my studies at Montana State University in the premed program. Hank had once pointed out to me when I caught him with pounds of pot, "You want to become an MD? What is the difference between what I do and what you would be doing? One is illegal and the other legal. What's the diff? They get addicted, and we both get paid."

He was right. I went to medical school and became a naturopathic physician instead of an emergency room physician.

—From a forthcoming book by
Valerie Lane Simonsen, N.D.
www.hoknowmore.com

MY GUARDIAN ANGEL IS A TRUCK DRIVER

It was just after 2:00 A.M. when Jacquelyn Lynn Diaz received an urgent call from the Hillsborough County sheriff's dispatch. A call had come in, reporting a disabled vehicle blocking the unbarricaded train crossing on Sidney Road, just west of Plant City. Arriving at the scene, she found a white Ford pickup loaded with cinder blocks and all four tires flat, sitting between the tracks. Pulling into the yard of the closest house, she was greeted by a young boy and his grandfather. The old man explained that he was the one that called in the abandoned vehicle report; he had watched two men stop the truck on the tracks, shut off the engine, get out, flatten the tires, and then run off in the direction of town.

Jacquelyn had been a deputy sheriff for five years. Working the midnight until eight in the morning shift, she had experienced her share of harrowing moments. However, this night would test even her resolve.

Jacquelyn called her dispatch and requested a tow truck to the scene to remove the vehicle from the tracks. Moments later, the dispatcher responded. The earliest that a tow truck would be available was an hour later; they were currently responding to a multivehicle accident with injuries on I-4. She needed to resolve the problem herself as fast as possible; the train to Jacksonville was scheduled to cross that intersection at 2:35 A.M. This night, the train was loaded with 240 tons of fertilizer—potassium phosphate, a highly corrosive substance, and ammonium nitrate, a lethal explosive—and deadly if combined.

Jacquelyn looked at the only two people that could possibly help and knew she was on her own. The grandfather was visibly weak and frail, and his grandson was much too young. Running to the truck, she found the doors locked. Breaking the driver's door window with her flashlight, she reached in and unlocked the door. Once inside, her stomach dropped—the steering wheel was locked, and the keys were not in the ignition. Getting out, she assessed the situation—it just got worse; the front wheels had been turned all the way to the left and were wedged tight between the rails.

She returned to her car and pulled it behind the truck. Lining her front bumper with the back of the truck, she attempted, to no avail, to push it from the tracks. Checking her watch, it was now 2:25 A.M., and she was rapidly running out of time. Calling her dispatch, she apprised them of her situation. She was told that, although there had been repeated attempts, as of that moment, they were still unable to contact the train crew. She absolutely had to move the abandoned vehicle from the tracks.

There was absolutely no way she could begin to evacuate all of the homes and businesses that would be affected if the train collided with the abandoned pickup. She was at her wit's end—standing in the middle of the road, she stared at the pickup. It was unconceivable to her that someone purposely abandoned the pickup on the tracks to cause an accident.

Turning around, she was face-to-face with the front bumper and massive grill of a Peterbilt. The truck's driver was standing next to her and was asking her a question that, for some reason, she just couldn't comprehend. Looking up at him, she asked, "What did you say?"

Smiling at her confusion, the young man with coal-black hair and bright blue eyes responded, "I just asked if you needed some help."

"Oh, thank God, yes I do." She quickly explained her situation to the driver. He understood and reacted immediately. Backing his rig up, he exchanged places with Jacquelyn as she drove her squad back to the old man's front yard. Stepping out of the cab, he opened his side compartment, grabbing a small sledgehammer and a large screwdriver. Breaking the passenger's door window, he opened the door and slid inside. Jacquelyn climbed in behind the steering wheel, eager to assist him in any way she could. Looking at her watch, it was now 2:32 A.M.—they had less than three minutes, give or take, until they would be forced to abandon the truck and run for their lives.

Setting the screwdriver against the ignition on the steering column, the driver smacked it resoundingly with the hammer. Shattering the lock, he pried the cover off and dropped it to the floor. One more hit, and he pulled the steering wheel as hard as he could, breaking the last locking pin and allowing the front wheels to begin to turn. Jacquelyn grabbed the steering wheel and pushed it to the right with all of her strength. The driver pulled, as Jacquelyn turned the steering wheel, until the front wheels were finally straight. The driver pushed Jacquelyn out of the truck as the crossings bells and flashing lights began. The train was one mile away.

Jacquelyn slammed the door to the pickup and ran to the far side of the road as the truck driver climbed into the cab of his truck. Easing his truck forward, he pressed his front bumper against the tailgate of the pickup and began to push. The pickup moved about a foot and stopped. The headlight of the approaching train was clearly visible, sweeping back and forth across the track ahead of it. The train's horn began to blare, one long blast—two short—one long. The train was less than a quarter of a mile away. The semi pushed the pickup again; this time the smaller truck lowered itself to the ground, like a wild animal readying to strike—the bed began to buckle—but still it did not move. The train's horn blared again, one long blast—a one second pause—then another long blast. The train was less than the distance of a football field away. The semi's engine roared as it slowly started moving the pickup forward, collapsing the bed and the back of the cab as it did. The train's horn began one long blast; it was only seconds now from the crossing. In one valiant effort, the semi accelerated, pushing the pickup across the second set of tracks. Only seconds before the train would have collided with it, the semi followed the pickup across the tracks to safety. The train shook the ground and whipped the stagnant air into frenzy as it whizzed past Jacquelyn—its horn blaring.

Jacquelyn stood transfixed as the train clattered into the night. After the last car passed, she looked up, expecting to see the semi and its driver on the other side of the tracks—but neither of them was there. She returned to the old man and asked if he had seen where the truck driver had gone, but he only shook his head. "That man risked his life; he deserves a commendation," Jacquelyn explained to the old man and his grandson. Again, the old man shook his head, "Miss, I didn't see no semi truck—or a driver—I only saw you."

Now, you would think that this is where the story should end—but, instead, this is only the beginning of Jacquelyn's story.

Jacquelyn knew that she was not crazy; there was a truck driver helping her that night, and she was going to find him. As she waited for the wrecker to arrive, she reexamined the interior and exterior of the pickup truck. The steering column was destroyed from the impact of the hammer and screwdriver. Both door glasses were broken out. The bed and cab were bent and deformed from being pushed. Jacquelyn knew she had not done this herself; someone—or something—had helped her.

Over the next two weeks, Jacquelyn made phone call after phone call. She contacted every trucking company within a two-hundred-mile radius of Plant City—all to no avail; not one company had a truck in that area that night. Knowing that there were millions of trucks from all over the continental United States, her truck could have originated from anywhere. She patrolled Highway 574 and U.S. 92 from Tampa to Plant City every night in hopes of running into the truck and its driver again.

Jacquelyn was into the second month of her search when she received a radio call from a fellow deputy wondering if she would be willing to meet him for lunch. Excited by the prospect that he had found some information regarding her unidentified truck, she agreed, and headed to the truck stop at the junction of I–4 and Wheeler Road. Once inside, she found him sitting in a corner booth in the "reserved for on-duty drivers" section. This was actually her first time inside the truck stop to eat. She had been there on a few occasions responding to disturbances, but she never took the time to frequent its restaurant—not even for coffee. The drivers gave her wary glances as she walked into their section but quickly went back to what they were doing, ignoring her and the other officer.

"Well?" she asked.

"Well, what?"

"I thought you might have some information for me."

"I just figured you would be hungry—and I also figured that you just couldn't see the forest for the trees. If you're looking for a truck, there is no better place to start than at a truck stop. Do you see your driver in here?"

She glanced around the room, but not a single face rang a bell. "No—he's not in here." Looking around, she discovered that the room was not just a section of the restaurant set aside for drivers, it was a shrine to truck drivers past and present. There were hundreds of baseball caps with company logos embroidered across the front hanging from hooks on the wall. There were door decals displayed on the back of each booth, from companies that were no longer in existence. Around the entire room were framed newspaper articles of truck-related stories. They covered a time span of the fifty years the truck stop was in business. Across from where they were sitting was a distinctive door decal at the back of an empty booth. She immediately recognized it; it was the same decal she had seen on her mystery truck two months before. Bold red letters on a black background read *RDT Inc* . . . Catching the eye of the waitress, Jacquelyn waved her over.

"You two ready to order?" the waitress asked.

"Not quite yet, but I was wondering what you could tell me about that decal over there," Jacquelyn said as she pointed to the empty booth across from them.

"Not much, that was long before my time. I have only worked here for a couple of years. The owner would know though." Looking at her watch, she said, "He should be here in about fifteen minutes."

Jacquelyn and her companion ordered coffee and sandwiches and waited. The two were just finishing their lunch when a short, rotund man approached their table. His watery-blue eyes were red-rimmed from lack of sleep, and he bent slightly at the waist almost in an apologetic attitude as he spoke. "I'm the owner; my name is Tom Davis. Charlotte said you wanted some information about one of our decals. I'll be glad to tell you—that is, if I know the answer."

Again Jacquelyn pointed to the empty booth across from them. "What can you tell me about that company?"

"It's no longer in business—hasn't been for going on twenty-five years."

"I'm positive I saw that same decal on a truck two months ago."

"Not that decal you didn't. No disrespect, but you're mistaken officer," Tom said. "Excuse me for a minute, and I'll show you what I mean."

Tom walked across the room to the far corner, reaching up; he gently took one of the framed newspaper articles from the wall and returned to Jacquelyn's table. Handing her the 8½ × 11-inch picture frame, he took a seat in the empty booth across from them and waited. Jacquelyn scanned the article quickly; there was a photograph of a derailed train and a destroyed semi-truck lying on its side. At the bottom was another, smaller photograph, this one of a compact car that was also involved in the accident. The headline read, "Local Driver, Ronald Davis, Killed in Spectacular Train Crash," and displayed a small picture of the same young man with black hair and blue eyes Jacquelyn had met two months before. Jacquelyn read the three-column article from the beginning.

Early Tuesday morning, at the unprotected rail crossing at the junction of Turkey Creek and Sidney Roads, an unidentified motorist ran his vehicle into a second automobile driven by eighteen-year-old Mary Anne Diaz, of Plant City, (See inset below) who was stopped behind a pickup truck driven by Kenneth Myers of Bradenton Florida. Both vehicles were stopped waiting for the train. The impact was so great according to witnesses; it pushed both Mr. Myers's and Ms. Diaz's vehicles onto the tracks in the path of the oncoming train. Ms. Diaz's vehicle was severely damaged, and unable to be moved from the tracks on its own. Mr. Myers made several attempts to open the doors to extricate the woman and her two-year-old daughter Jacquelyn, who was buckled into a car seat. Mr. Myers reported at the scene, that Ms. Diaz, slumped over the steering wheel, was unresponsive and bleeding from a wound on her forehead.

"Ronald Davis of RDT Trucking pulled his truck loaded with grain on to the accident scene a few minutes later. He made several attempts to help Mr. Myers and other bystanders pry open Ms. Diaz's door, but the young woman and her daughter were trapped inside. Mr. Myers told this reporter that he heard sirens in the distance, but they were racing the train, and he knew the train was closer. Mr. Myers attempted to drive his vehicle off of the tracks, but it too would not start.

"Mr. Myers guided Davis's truck behind Ms. Diaz's automobile in an attempt to push both vehicles to safety. Davis pushed Ms. Diaz's vehicle until it rested against the rear bumper of Mr. Myers's pickup. The train horn blared, as Davis began pushing both vehicles to safety. Once the vehicle belonging to Ms. Diaz crossed safely to the far side of the tracks, Davis apparently attempted to maneuver his rig out and around the two stalled vehicles, but, before it could clear the tracks, the train broadsided the trailer dragging Davis and his truck over a quarter-mile before the train derailed, and Davis's truck exploded into flames. According to Hillsborough County Coroner, Patricia Kenny, Ronald Davis appeared to have died instantly on impact."

Jacquelyn was at a loss for words; she passed the picture frame to her companion and looked at Tom Davis, who was still watching her. Tom was the first to speak, "Ronnie was my son."

"I'm Jacquelyn Diaz; my mother is Mary Anne. I was in the car with my mother that night."

—Lee Strong

BABE

It was the pride of the fleet—a beautiful new 1971 Kenworth cab-over. It was one truck out of a small fleet of seven based out of Denver, Colorado, special ordered for the company's top driver. Metallic green with white stripes, all aluminum wheels, an 8v 71 Detroit diesel engine, even air-conditioning. In 1971, it was better than most trucks on the road and turned a lot of heads. The lucky driver, Adron, was a World War II vet. He was speechless when John and his wife, Sally, the trucking company owners, handed him the keys and said she's yours to drive for all the years you have given us.

Adron babied the truck like no other, keeping her polished and washed. She was a source of praise and envy at his favorite truck stops. The truck ran flawlessly and was always seen on I-80 between Denver and Chicago hauling meat. One day, Adron missed his morning check call. By the evening check call, Sally told all the drivers to look for Adron as he seemed to be missing. He was found the following morning in North Platte, Nebraska, dead in his sleeper of an apparent heart attack. John and Sally were grief-stricken at the loss of their friend. After some debate over permits, John hauled Adron to his final resting place on a flatbed pulled by the truck Adron so loved. It was a fitting funeral for a good man.

After the funeral, John parked the truck out back and let it sit. He didn't want anyone else to drive it. By the winter of 1971, John and Sally realized they couldn't afford to keep a $35,000 truck parked any longer. About that time Dave walked into the office. Dave worked for a company down the road and had seen the sharp Kenworth sitting out back, doing nothing, and thought he would ask about a job driving it. John gave him a try after checking with his other drivers to see if they wanted Adron's truck. Hearing six no-thank-you's, he assigned the truck to Dave, who was thrilled.

John told him that a man died in the truck, but Dave replied, "I guess I'm not as superstitious as your other drivers." Dave took good care of the truck and nicknamed it Babe, but as the weather got colder things started to happen. One very cold morning in January of 1972, Dave showed up for his run at 2:00 A.M. to find Babe idling in the parking lot, all warmed up and ready to go. When he made his morning check call, he told Sally to thank whoever it was that started his truck for him as it was nice to have it all warmed up. Sally relayed the message to John and the mechanic, who didn't know what she was talking about. The next week the same thing happened again, only Dave didn't have to leave until 8:00 A.M. He went to the shop and thanked the mechanic once again for warming up his truck, but the mechanic said it must have been someone else. The same answer came from the office, which started everyone to wondering who was starting Babe.

After several more occurrences of the truck-starting events, Dave began to become agitated, as he thought one of the drivers was playing a trick on him to make him think his truck was haunted. Not liking to be the brunt of somebody's joke, he wrote a note on the company board warning everyone that he would eventually find out who it was, so the culprit should give up now and take his punishment. The note was kind of a joke, but serious in nature, too, as he was getting tired of the prank. Then the truck began starting at truck stops hundreds of miles from home.

John took it to Kenworth, who, after half a day's investigation, said we can't find anything wrong. Dave was assigned a load for Rapid City, South Dakota, leaving on June 9, 1972, to be delivered at 2:00 A.M. on June 10. Dave left Denver early on the 9th so he could take his time. By the time he got into northeast Wyoming at the junction of Highways 18 and 85, it was raining cats and dogs. Dave decided to pull Babe off to the side of the road, take a nap, and get up about midnight to go the rest of the way to Rapid City. Maybe the weather would calm down by then, he thought, as he turned Babe off.

His alarm didn't go off, and he woke up at about 1:00 A.M. He bolted out of the sleeper and jumped into the driver's seat and tried to start Babe. She wouldn't even crank. Damn it, he said, knowing full well he was gonna be late for his delivery and probably miss his backhaul. He tried frantically to start the truck in the dark. No luck. He knew there was a ranch house about a mile away but decided to wait until first light before trying to find it.

At about 6:00 A.M., he walked to the ranch house to ask if he could use their phone. He called Sally, and, when she found out it was him, she began to cry. Dave asked, "What's wrong?"

She said, "We thought we lost you, Dave." She handed the phone to John, who told him the bad news.

"From what we hear, Dave, Rapid City was wiped out last night. Sounds like a dam broke." Dave was shocked.

John told him he would try to get help to him as soon as he could. The rancher gave Dave a ride back to the truck. He said, "I know a thing or two about trucks. Why don't you try to start it again while I have a look at her?"

Dave jumped into the seat. Under his breath he said, "C'mon, Babe," and turned the key. Babe roared to life like nothing was wrong. Dave went numb realizing that if his alarm clock would have gone off like it should have, and if Babe would have started, he would probably be dead.

The Rapid City flood took 238 lives that morning. For some reason, it seemed Babe kept the death toll from being 239. Babe ran flawlessly for the next four years. John and Sally told Dave it was time to trade her off. Dave said, "Like hell, you will. Name your price," and he bought her that day. In later years, she ended up in Dave's back lot looking tired and old. He never did sell Babe. He said, "They will bury me in that old truck."

—Gary M. Vaughn

PART 3

Haunted Highways: Legends and Lore of the Road

Phantom hitchhikers, roads haunted by spirits of the dead who peer into car windows, ghostly guardians protecting land from trespassers and thrill seekers—it seems there's no shortage of ghost legends and haunted lore about America's highways and byways. Hasn't everyone, when driving on a deserted road late at night, gotten a sudden chill and glanced quickly in the rear view mirror, even though they know there's nothing to be afraid of? Unless, of course, they happen to be driving on one of the bedeviled back roads described in the following pages. . .

ALABAMA PROM GIRL GHOST

Hey, this is Creole Williams from Hamilton, Alabama. Let me tell you about a ghost story from over between Natural Bridge and Jasper, Alabama, on Highway 5 around Nauvoo. A young girl had been to the prom with her boyfriend. It was a rainy, foggy night. Afterward, they were on their way home and got into a fight. She told him to let her out; she would walk. Walking down the side of the road, she was struck by a truck driver. He didn't stop. She was found the next day, dead in the ditch. From then on, if you're driving a truck down Highway 5 at night, and it's dark and rainy, they say she will climb on your step and ride looking in at you to see if you were the one who ran over her. Now, I'm not saying that I saw her, but I do believe in it. I have a friend who was actually trucking through there on a regular basis when the accident happened.

About three years ago, I was on my way home. It was about midnight, raining and foggy, and I cut through Highway 5 on a shortcut home—never looked out my window, but I could feel something peering through the window at me. I haven't been through there at night since.

—Josh "Creole" Williams

BLACK DOG

I am a trucker. This incident took place in 2001 or 2002. I do not remember exactly which month, but the weather was no longer cold. I was driving north on I–81 in Tennessee, around mile marker 30. It was late at night. The weather was clear, but there was no moon.

It came out of nowhere. It crossed in front of my truck from left to right at a rapid speed. It was not well defined in its shape but appeared to have silvery-black hair—bushy hair—and looked like a large dog. I didn't see any eyes, nose, or teeth. I saw it for just a split second—then it disappeared below my hood, disappearing from sight. I thought I ran over whatever it was, but heard no sound. I stopped to look for outward damage, but saw nothing. It was like I never saw or hit anything.

When I got home in the morning, I asked the mechanics to look under the truck for blood and hair. Nothing was found. I told them I thought I hit a dog. They said, "No, you didn't hit anything." I forgot about this incident until I was talking to another driver about long drives, late nights, and heavy eyelids while at the wheel. He told me about the "black dog" that drivers who are really tired sometimes see at night. He told me it was a harbinger of death, meaning: "Park now and sleep, or die in the wreck waiting for you just up the road."

I've been so tired I have blanked out for a few seconds more times than I can remember, but I never saw the black dog before this incident and have never seen it since.

—Jeff T.

BLONDIE

My uncle Jim, a truck driver, tells me that there is a rest area at mile marker 253 or 254 in Oklahoma where supposedly a woman nicknamed Blondie was found dead and still haunts the place.

Or you may have heard about mile marker 30 in Michigan, which was reported to be built over an Indian burial ground. (I am unsure about what highway.) Jim says if you do get stories about these areas they are very probably true since he has had many a trucker friend tell him of experiences of trucks being shaken violently (like someone is jumping on them) at both locations. He knows many truckers who refuse to stop at these rest areas altogether.

—Stacy Eldridge

LOVERS' LANE LEGEND

I have heard this one with a different twist to it in different parts of the country, but anyway, this is how we heard it when I was thirteen years old or so . . . Not so long ago, on a very rarely traveled river road on the outskirts of my hometown, a sixteen-year-old took his date to above said road for a little "alone" time. After being on the road for three to four miles, the car ran out of gas. The kid was always meaning to get the fuel gauge fixed but kept putting it off, as money was tight. After some heavy teenage romance, he informed his date he would walk to the nearest farmer's house for gas and instructed her to keep the doors locked in his absence.

Hours passed, and before her falling asleep in the darkness of night, she heard branches scraping the roof of the car. She thought this was strange, as there were trees nearby, but they were all very tall. Finally, sleep came anyway.

When she was awakened by police officers in the morning daylight, they informed her not to turn around and look, but curiosity got the best of her. When she looked, she saw the corpse of her boyfriend, his feet bound and tied to a tall tree branch, the breeze swinging his lifeless body, his fingernails scraping the top of the car, his face all bloody and mangled from the crows who had started their work. The killer was never apprehended . . .

Just a footnote: I scared many a date into my arms telling this story at night parked on that river road.

—Brian J. Nolan

RESURRECTION MARY: THE STORY OF THE VANISHING HITCHHIKER

illow Springs, Illinois, is a quiet suburb situated twenty miles outside of Chicago. It's the backdrop for the legend of Resurrection Mary. Growing up in Willow Springs, I believed that the ghost of Mary was a local legend, the kind that every town might have. As an adult, I came to understand that Mary's story was in fact one of the most popular Chicago-area ghost stories of all time.

My grandma first shared the story of Mary with my brothers and me when we were in grade school. She said that in the late 1930s, Mary was about twenty years old and lived with her parents in their Willow Springs home. One evening, she and her boyfriend went to the local dance hall, the Oh Henry Ballroom. Located near Willow Springs Road on Archer Avenue, the dance hall remains open to this day, but the name has changed to the Willowbrook Ballroom. That evening at the dance hall, Mary got into an argument with her boyfriend and stormed out of the dance hall. She wandered onto Archer Avenue to hitchhike for a ride home. Tragically, she was struck by a car and left to die. When her parents and boyfriend learned of Mary's death, they were devastated. They held funeral services for her and buried her body in Resurrection Cemetery on Archer Avenue, just miles from the place that she was killed.

My grandma said that from the time of Mary's death, there were countless reported sightings of Mary's ghost. Most times, her ghost has been seen wandering on Archer Avenue. She is consistently described as a pretty, blond-haired, blue-eyed young woman wearing 1930s-style clothing. Her figure appears and disappears into thin air.

During my teenage years, my friends and I frequently shared stories of the legend of Resurrection Mary. From several different friends, I recall hearing the story of a man who had spent an entire evening with Mary's ghost during the 1950s. As the legend goes, the man met a woman fitting Mary's description while he was at a dance hall in Chicago. He introduced himself, and they danced together for several hours. She was cold to the touch and quiet, he said. At the end of the evening, she hailed a cab, and he never heard from her again. The woman asked the cab driver to drive her out of the city and drop her in front of Resurrection Cemetery. When she got out of the cab, the cab driver said she disappeared without a trace.

Especially around Halloween during my teenage years, it was common for my friends and me to drive around in search of Mary's ghost. We'd drive by Resurrection Cemetery in hopes to catch a glimpse of her. Several people said that their cars mysteriously stalled in front of Resurrection Cemetery. The cemetery itself was said to be haunted. At one time, the gates of the cemetery were bent and scorched as if someone was locked in and trying to get out. We'd also drive around speculating which house belonged to Mary and her parents. Legend has it that after Mary's death, her parents went crazy with grief and let the home deteriorate to shambles.

This is the legend of Resurrection Mary as I came to know it growing up in Willow Springs, Illinois. The legend has been widely reported and studied for factual basis. Whether one believes it or not, it is certainly one of the greatest Chicago-area ghost stories of all time.

—Melissa Neddermeyer

MOTHER AND BABY APPARITION

When I was in training with my OTR mentor, I heard this story. A rookie driver was on his way to Chicago from Los Angeles, headed north on U.S. 54 from Moriarty, New Mexico. In a typical rookie mistake, he got off at the wrong exit. His trainer was in the sleeper. Instead of bypassing the small town of Moriarty, he had to go through it. The new driver was half-asleep and fighting to stay awake. As he gets halfway through town, he did a micronap. As he opened his eyes, he saw a young lady about twenty-five years old standing in front of him, in the middle of the road, holding an infant. He slammed on his brakes—but it was too late. He hit her, and she fell under the truck. He pulled his brakes and screamed at his trainer, "I just hit someone!" as he bailed out the door to render aid.

The rookie ran around the front of the truck, afraid of what he might see. Nothing. His trainer bailed out in only his underwear. (It was about 2:00 A.M.) He looked under the truck. Both of them looked frantically for the lady or the baby. The trainer said, "Are you sure you hit them?"

The driver said, "Yeah, I felt the bump." But as they continued to look, a local police officer pulled up behind them. He walks up and says, "What's the problem?"

The rookie started to explain. The officer stopped him and said, "Let me guess. The woman was in a dark dress. Baby in a white wrap?"

"Right," he said. "Thank God, I missed her."

The police officer says, "Yeah, by about twenty-eight years." Then he explained that in 1960, a young lady was walking home on the same road. She was run over by a trucker that had fallen asleep at the wheel, killing her and the baby she was carrying. And ever since, she has roamed the road, scaring drivers that were asleep or not paying attention.

—Jim Bradshaw

QUANTUM HITCHHIKER IN EL RENO

El Reno, Oklahoma—If you are traveling on Route 66 between Weatherford and El Reno, Oklahoma, at night, keep your eyes open because legend has it that this part of the old Mother Road is haunted by an elderly humped-back man. Said to appear in a brown trench coat, wearing a Bogie-style hat pulled down over his eyes, he has often been spotted walking along the old highway, especially on foggy or rainy nights. Reportedly, one person picked this old figure up one wet evening and the eerie little man wouldn't talk to him. Soon, the vagabond tried to jump out of the moving car. The driver immediately pulled over to the side and let him out, only to spot the man walking again ahead of the driver several miles on down the road. Another person said that they thought they had hit the man with their vehicle, but when they stopped to check on him, no one was there. Do you believe it? Keep your eyes peeled.

—Kathy Weiser

THE BLOODY BRIDE BRIDGE

U nless you're a native of central Wisconsin, you're probably not familiar with the Bloody Bride Bridge and the
specter that haunts it. I wasn't either, until my first se-
mester at UW-Stevens Point.

It was my librarian friend, Alice, an older women who not
only offered great literary recommendations, but who also had a
mental archive of the haunted legends woven throughout Stevens Point's history, who first told me about the legend of the
Bloody Bride Bridge.

The reputed history, she whispered to me as we stood in the
third floor stacks, is that a young bride was killed in an auto accident on Highway 66, on her wedding night. However, the Stevens Point Police Department has no record of a bride ever having
been killed on that road.

Sometime after the alleged accident, a police officer driving
down Highway 66 suddenly slammed on his brakes to avoid
colliding with a young woman dressed in white who had wandered into the middle of the road. But he wasn't quick enough.
There was no thud, no impact at all, but he knew he had driven
his vehicle into her. When the squad car finally came to a dead

stop, he looked for the woman he had run down—but there was no body, no bloodshed.

Confused and concluding that he hadn't been getting enough sleep lately, the police officer climbed back into his vehicle and sat behind the steering wheel. When he turned the key in the ignition, he checked his rearview mirror and saw the reflection of the Bloody Bride, sitting in his backseat.

The rumor, Alice said, is that if you park your car on the Bloody Bride Bridge, at midnight the bride will appear in your vehicle.

I thought about the legend for weeks, and when Halloween rolled around, the opportunity simply stared me in the face. I had convinced my boyfriend to abandon the party town of Oshkosh for a weekend, enticing him with the legend of the Bloody Bride, and we, along with my sister, who wasn't thrilled about having to sit in the backseat, drove out to the bridge on Highway 66.

The moon peeked over the black spires of the pines, lighting the world just enough so that everything in it was a silhouette. We parked on the bridge overlooking the Plover River. Even the water was dark and silent, stealthily winding its way beneath us. With the exception of one set of passing headlights, the night was empty and devoid of life. We waited in silence as the digital numbers on the radio turned to 12:00 A.M. We stared down the straight stretch of road, illuminated only by our dim headlights and dissolving into the pitch. But the Bloody Bride never wandered out, nor was she sitting next to my sister in the backseat.

A quarter of an hour passed. Our pulses slowed, and the sweat evaporated from the backs of our necks as we realized that the legend of the Bloody Bride was just that—a legend.

Not even requiring nods of acquiescence, my boyfriend turned the key in the ignition and I cranked the heat. Even though I had been holding my hands close to my body, they had turned to ice. The radio came back on, but every channel was static. It screeched like a metal screw scraping down a glass pane as I twisted the dial to shut it off.

My boyfriend switched the brights on.

And there she stood, in the middle of the road, as though she had been there the entire time, waiting, daring us to accelerate forward. Her appearance was so palpable, so tragically lifelike that, if I had not known the legend, I would have sworn that she was the victim of an accident that had happened only seconds before. But it had been decades. Blood matted her dark hair to her scalp and soiled her lace bodice. A scarlet laceration across her chest marked where the seat belt had carved into her flesh. One leg appeared broken, bent at an awkward angle, and yet she stood.

Before I could brace myself, the car was careening backward down Highway 66. Shadows whooshed past. My head was pinned to the headrest. I could only stare straight ahead at the Bloody Bride, who graced the bridge.

The tires screamed on the asphalt as my boyfriend wrenched the car into a U-turn. We raced back to Stevens Point, likely shattering the speed limit, but we all knew that we had to get as far from that bridge as possible.

I've never returned to the Bloody Bride Bridge, and I don't

think I ever will. There's no doubt in my mind that she is still there, however, and even though it might be Halloween, or just another night of working on the road, it's always her wedding night.

—Hannah Morrissey

HITCHHIKER IN RED

This happened in 1993. I lived in Colorado's San Luis Valley at the time and was talking to the Questa chief of police about their investigation into a local bull-mutilation case. During the course of our conversation, I asked about other reports of the unusual. The chief of police hesitated, then out of the blue he told me this peculiar tale.

A close relative, an uncle, had been driving home late at night, north of Questa on Highway 522, on Easter weekend. He was about seven or eight miles out of Questa, heading south, when he spotted "a woman hitchhiker dressed up in red," walking along the side of the highway. Naturally, he stopped to see if she needed help or a ride into town. He stopped, and without a word, she climbed into the pickup and sat next to him on the truck's bench seat, silently looking straight ahead. As he pulled back onto the road, he turned to ask her why she was walking along the road alone so late at night. It was then he noticed she had "goat's legs and cloven hooves." Before the startled man could react to the sight, she dematerialized from his front seat.

To me, this story sounded like a *Twilight Zone* rerun. But according to the police chief, his uncle is extremely "honest and stable—he wouldn't make up such an outrageous story for any reason." The police chief said they tried to talk his uncle out of making a report, but he insisted. As I discovered when researching my first book, *The Mysterious Valley,* stories of "Old Scratch," or the urban devil, are still circulating through northern New Mexico and southern Colorado

—Christopher O'Brien
Investigative Journalist/Anomalist
www.ourstrangeplanet.com

This is adapted from a story that originally appeared in the book Secrets of the Mysterious Valley *by Christopher O'Brien, Adventures Unlimited Press, 2007.*

DEVIL'S PROMENADE AND THE
HORNET SPOOK LIGHT

Bobbing and bouncing along a dirt road in northeast Oklahoma is the Hornet Spook Light, a paranormal enigma for more than a century. Described most often as an orange ball of light, the orb travels from east to west along a four-mile gravel road, long called the Devil's Promenade by area locals.

The spook light, often referred to as the Joplin Spook Light or the Tri-State Spook Light, is actually in Oklahoma near the small town of Quapaw. However, it is most often seen from the east, which is why it has been "attached" to the tiny hamlet of Hornet, Missouri, and the larger, better-known town of Joplin.

According to the legend, the spook light was first seen by Indians along the infamous Trail of Tears in 1836; however, the first "official" report occurred in 1881 in a publication called the *Ozark Spook Light*.

The ball of fire, described as varying from the size of a baseball to a basketball, dances and spins down the center of the road at high speeds, rising and hovering above the treetops before it retreats and disappears. Others have said it sways from side to side, like a lantern being carried by some invisible force.

In any event, the orange firelike ball has reportedly been appearing nightly for well over a hundred years. According to locals, the best time to view the spook light is between the hours of 10:00 P.M. and midnight, and it tends to shy away from large groups and loud sounds.

Though many paranormal and scientific investigators have studied the light, including the Army Corps of Engineers, no one has been able to provide a conclusive answer as to the origin of the light.

Many explanations have been presented over the years, including escaping natural gas, reflecting car lights and billboards, and will-o'-the-wisps, a luminescence created by rotting organic matter. However, all of these explanations fall short of being conclusive.

As to the theory of escaping natural gas, which is common in marshy areas, the Hornet Spook Light is seemingly not affected by wind or by rain, and how would it self-ignite? The idea that it might be a will-o'-the-wisp is discounted, as this biological phenomenon does not display the intensity of the ball of light seen along the Devil's Promenade Road. Explanations of headlights or billboards are easily discarded, as the light was seen years before automobiles or billboards were made and before a road even existed in the area.

One possible explanation that is not as easily discounted, but not yet proven conclusive, is that the lights are electrical atmospheric charges. In areas where rocks, deep below the earth's surface, are shifting and grinding, an electrical charge can be created.

This area, lying on a fault line running east from New Madrid, Missouri, westward to Oklahoma was the site of four earthquakes during the eighteenth century. These types of electrical fields are most commonly associated with earthquakes.

Other interesting legends also abound about the light that provide a more ghostly explanation. The oldest is the story of a Quapaw Indian maiden who fell in love with a young brave. However, her father would not allow her to marry the man as he did not have a large enough dowry. The pair eloped but were soon pursued by a party of warriors. According to the legend, when the couple was close to being apprehended, they joined hands above the Spring River and leaped to their deaths. It was shortly after this event that the light began to appear and was attributed to the spirits of the young lovers.

Another legend tells of a miner whose cabin was attacked by Indians while he was away. Upon his return, he found his wife and children missing and is said to continue looking for them along the old road, searching with his lantern.

Others say the spook light is the ghost of an Osage Indian chief who was decapitated in the area and continues to search for his lost head, with a lantern held high in his hand.

Sightings of the spook light are common, sometimes even reported to be seen inside vehicles. A few people who have been walking along the road at night have even claimed to feel the heat of the ball as it passed near them.

Reportedly, the moving anomaly, growing brighter and dimmer, larger and smaller, can be seen approximately twelve miles southwest of Joplin, Missouri. To get to Devil's Promenade Road, take Interstate 44 west from Joplin but, before you reach the Oklahoma border, take the next-to-the-last Missouri exit onto Star Route 43. Traveling south for about four miles, you will reach a crossroads—the Devil's Promenade Road.

—Kathy Weiser

www.legendsofamerica.com

THE THIRTEEN TREES AT LOUISVILLE'S HOT ROD HAVEN

Born and bred in Louisville, Kentucky, I have heard several tales from haunted train trestles to supernatural dogs chasing cars on the road to an old TB hospital. But I think the one that stands out the most is Hot Rod Haven—a curvy stretch of wooded road that passes by a cemetery and ends with a large curve to a major drop-off.

The cemetery itself is a legend all its own with stories galore, from a statue of the Virgin Mary crying to broken headless statues being seen with their heads to people being tossed across the property. But back to Hot Rod Haven.

At one time (it has been a while since I went down the road), there were thirteen trees that were marked with red paint. The thirteenth tree resembled Satan's face, you know, within the nature of the bark. The legend was, if you did not count all thirteen trees, at the end of the road where it curved with the drop-off, you would crash on that turn. Also, it was said that on Halloween at a specific time (I don't recall hearing the time), you could drive down the road and see a group of people, those who died in wrecks, walking the road. As they approached the thirteenth tree, they would disappear.

—Shari McPeek

GHOST DOGS OF WAVERLY HILLS SANATORIUM

A local landmark here in Louisville, which has been featured on *TAPS* and *Scariest Places,* is a place called Waverly Hills Sanatorium. In the past couple of years, it was purchased and is being restored and brought back to its original condition. It's used during the Halloween season as a haunted house.

There are legends of the top floor being haunted by a nurse who killed herself—some say because she was pregnant by a married doctor; other stories say she did it because she was pregnant and afraid the baby would be infected. To give some additional history, there is a "body chute" on the premises. It was used to keep the patients' morale up—staff would take those who had died and slide them down the body chute out the back of the facility so patients could not see the great numbers of those dead. Also, I say "slide" because the corridor, or tunnel, has stairs on one side for the living and flat-angled concrete for the departed. (Basically, the living would walk down and slide the body next to them.)

But back in the day the original owners hired a groundskeeper to keep out teens who wanted to walk the crumbling corridors and travel down the body chute. The groundskeeper lived on the premises in a little trailer and had these three dogs that he would let roam the property. As time went on, it came to be that the dogs' bodies were taken over by the ghosts of those who felt disrespected by people who made their tragedy a form of entertainment.

The possessed dogs were white, with red glowing eyes. Every time someone would attempt the "Hill" (the location is up on a hill), sometimes going up and sometimes going down, the dogs would come out and chase you. There were three of them, and, yes, they barked, growled, showed their teeth, and foamed at the mouth. Think of the worst dog image you have seen with rabies and then give it red eyes.

I had friends who swore that upon leaving one night, the dogs came after them. Even after hitting them with their car, the dogs got up and continued to chase them, then disappeared at the end of the property.

—Shari McPeek

KENTUCKY TRAIN TRACK MONSTER

As the story goes, people who have crossed the train tracks in Jefferson County, Kentucky, looking for the Pope Lick Monster would rather fall from the tracks than to face it. The monster, named after Pope Lick Creek, which the train bridge crosses, is also known as the Goat Man.

The specific tale as I heard it is that there was a kid who went looking for the monster. The boy fell to his death—the mystery train came with its ghost passengers and shook the tracks, and he fell. Every full moon, you can ride by and hear the train and feel the ground rumble. If you stop and walk back to the tracks, you can see a boy struggling to stay on the moving tracks, screaming for help until he falls to the ground below and disappears. I heard you never see the train, just a light from the engine. The big story is that if you are on the bridge when this event happens, you too will fall, and the train collects another passenger for its never-ending voyage.

We did go out to the site several times looking for the train and the boy. When we did not see anything, we turned to the monster, thinking maybe the train was just a legend, but perhaps the boy was actually pushed by the monster. But we really never saw or heard anything.

We did notice that it was strange that some of the surrounding land had animal paths from the tracks to the woods and that the plant life was eaten and animal bones were found throughout the area, but we are talking woods here and there are deer and other animals throughout. But saying it was "the monster" was so much cooler at the time. As for getting on the tracks, that would be a "NO." My dad works for the railroad, and if he ever caught me or my friends doing something like that . . . put it this way, I would welcome seeing the Goat Man over that punishment.

The only story I heard about the monster's creation is unlike all the others I have read. It brings in another tale and location— the Bell Witch from Tennessee, located close to the Kentucky border. I heard that she created the boy to terrorize the Bell family and those who did her wrong, but he broke free from her and came to Kentucky. To pay penance for his bad deeds and unholy creation, he roams the railroad site as a guardian of the tracks, trying to scare thrill seekers away from a horrible death. Those who don't know his mission take his actions (screaming, throwing things, etc.) as a threat instead of a warning, and that is why his legend as a monster grows.

—Shari McPeek

GHOST OF THE HIGHWAY MAN

The *Arizona Republic* newspaper has written articles pertaining to a highway that the locals call Blood Alley. There is another published article about the tragic death of a family of six along this highway. I am not sure of the year that this happened, but I believe it was around 1992–93, either in August or September.

Blood Alley is a desolate, narrow, two-lane highway that runs from Wickenburg, through Wikieup, and down into Kingman, Arizona. It is a winding, hilly road filled with blind curves and almost no road shoulder room. Due to the hills, there are dead zones where cell phones don't work, and there is no radio reception except static. Oftentimes, you can travel the entire length of this road without ever seeing another vehicle.

The entire length of this highway is dotted with small white crosses. Some crosses are spaced at different intervals; some are in a series; and some are clusters that mark where an entire vehicle of people have died tragically.

There is one particular spot that is marked by six white crosses. A family of six, traveling in a station wagon with a hitched trailer, was moving from California to Arizona. Along the way, a rear tire blew, and the father pulled his vehicle as far off the road as he could. He got out and set flares in front and back of the vehicle to warn other drivers. The father had just jacked up the car and had stepped behind the trailer to retrieve something. That's when he was plowed into by a pickup truck. The pickup hit with such force that it pushed the trailer into the back of the station wagon, killing the four children sitting in the back, all the way to the front, where the wife was sitting, who was also killed. The car then caught on fire. The youngest child was only six months old. The driver of the pickup sustained severe injuries but survived. Every time I have passed this spot, I've always said a little prayer for the family that died there.

Members of my family and I have traveled this road often on our way to Las Vegas and back home. On one such trip in 1992 or 1993, we had a strange experience that we've come to call "The Highway Man."

My husband Sam* and I, along with my brother and sister-in-law, were coming back from a family reunion in Las Vegas. As is usual with our family reunions, we delayed in leaving because it was so hard to say good-bye. We finally left Vegas late at night for our return trip home. Since our pickup was having engine problems, we decided that we would drive ahead, with my brother following behind us. That way, if our pickup had problems, we could catch a ride with my brother and his wife and not be stranded out in the middle of nowhere in the dead of night.

It was between two and three in the morning, the air was chilly, the moon was out, and the stars were shining brightly. I had just commented to my husband how bright the stars were without the glare of city lights. The moon was just bright enough to illuminate the landscape and the many white crosses. Up ahead, the road began a gentle bank to the right. I turned around to see if my brother was still behind us and estimated that he was a little more than half a mile behind us.

When I turned to face front, I noticed a small white light ahead. It reminded me of a flashlight. I said to my husband, "Do you see that light up there? Looks like a flashlight, doesn't it?"

"Yeah," he said. "Looks kind of like a flashlight."

"God, I hope it's not an accident or someone stranded," I said. "How awful. Slow down, Sam, in case we need to help someone."

My husband began to slow down. As we got closer to the light, we saw that it looked more like a kerosene lantern—the kind you use for camping.

"That doesn't look like a flashlight. Looks more like a lantern," my husband commented.

"Yeah. Isn't that strange? Why would anyone be out here camping?" I wondered aloud. "And so close to the road? That doesn't make sense. Could someone be out there camping and walked to the road? Maybe their flashlight went out and they had to use a lantern."

Just as we came abreast of the light, a man stepped out of the shadows. I could make out that he was a little over six feet tall, dressed in a black duster, jeans, and cowboy boots. He had on a black cowboy hat that was pulled down low, concealing his face. He held the lantern in front of him, just above his head. From the glow of the lantern, I could see an old-time black Harley parked behind him and off to his right side. I remember him taking one step forward, and, as we passed him, he took one step back, disappearing into the shadows. The light went out.

"Holy cats! Did you see that? Did you see that?" I shouted. I had turned around and was facing the back of the pickup. "I don't see the light! Where's the light! Oh my God! Where did he go?"

At the same time I was yelling at my husband, he was yelling, "I'm not stopping! I'm not stopping! I don't care who the hell that was or what they needed, I'm not stopping!"

I kept facing backward, looking for my brother Toby's car headlights. I kept waiting . . . and soon panic set in.

"I don't see Toby's car," I said. "Something's happened! We have to turn back. Slow down and find a place where we can turn around! I don't see him!" As my husband began slowing down and searching for a place to turn around, my brother's car appeared. Relieved at seeing his car, all of us continued the trip into Wickenburg.

At Wickenburg, we pulled in and parked at a McDonald's parking lot. We had just barely parked the vehicles when all of us piled out, talking all at once: "Did you see that?" . . . "What was that?" . . . "What did you see?"

I told my brother, "You go first. Tell me what you saw."

Toby and his wife, Maggie, began to describe that they saw our taillights disappear around a right bend in the road. As they came to the bend, they noticed a light up ahead that looked like a flashlight shining. Maggie had told my brother, "Slow down, baby. It looks like there is someone up ahead with a flashlight. I think it might be Fran and Sam."

Toby began slowing down, he told us. "As I was slowing down, we noticed that it wasn't a flashlight that we saw. It looked more like a lantern. You know, the kind you take camping. Maggie said she didn't remember you having a lantern with you.

"All of a sudden," my brother continued, "I saw a tall man step out, holding the lantern in front of him. I think I saw a Harley next to him. Maggie saw more than I did."

Maggie picked up the story. "We saw the light and thought it was you guys. I told Toby to slow down, just in case. As we came closer to the light, I could see that it was a lantern. I remarked to your brother that it was odd that you guys had a lantern with you. We slowed way down, and, as we passed, this man stepped out. He was tall, about six foot. He had on a black duster, jeans, and cowboy boots. Oh yeah, he also had on a black cowboy hat. I couldn't see his face. He held the lantern out in front of him. I also saw a black Harley. An old one, like the bikers ride. When we went past him, he took one step back and disappeared. So did the light. I started screaming at your brother, 'Go, baby, go! Don't stop! Don't stop!'"

My brother said at that point he just floored the gas pedal and tried to get out of there as fast as he could.

It took us about an hour to calm down enough to be able to continue our drive into Phoenix. During that hour, we compared notes and went over the experience dozens of times. It was very frightening that all of us, traveling in two separate vehicles, experienced the same thing in exactly the same way.

After that night, I researched for a while to find out who that man might be and what could have happened. But I turned up nothing. There have been so many tragic deaths on that road that names and circumstances are lost in time.

Eventually, we named the incident "The Highway Man." Even to this day, when I think about that night, my heart races, my hands start to shake, and my palms sweat. I can clearly see that night in my mind . . . and I get scared all over again.

—Frances Tasho-Pullen

*Some names have been changed to protect privacy.

OLD HIGHWAY 666 IN NEW MEXICO

The old Highway 666 in New Mexico is a long, desolate highway out in the middle of nowhere. There's not even any homes, rest areas, or buildings on this stretch—truly spooky, especially at night. I drove that highway several times before they changed the highway number. I always hoped that nothing bad would happen to me while I drove on it and couldn't wait to get off it.

Drivers must make sure to have plenty of fuel before they head down this long stretch. I saw a few trucks and one or two cars, but nothing much out there. A motorist should always be able to count on a trucker to help them if they are broke down on the road. We see everything while we are driving. Just hope it's a good trucker, and not one that can take a girl in the sleeper bunk, rape her, kill her, then dump her body by the side of the road. This has happened with a few truckers out there. Serial killers. They mostly pick up young women hitchhikers or lot lizards (prostitutes).

On this highway, people have reported seeing the following: an apparition of a car that apparently drives motorists off the road, but only on nights with a full moon; a crazed man in a tractor-trailer who tries to run people over; and a pack of ghost dogs that have allegedly run across cars and cut the tires with their sharp teeth.

I have also heard that a 1960s muscle car shows up at night right behind people, coming out of nowhere, and follows right on their bumper. The motorist who's being followed often speeds up, and this is where I think that many crashes happen. They are trying to get away from the car on their bumper. The car on the bumper does not pass them, but eventually slows down and then goes out of sight.

The most well-known legends and stories told about this section of the highway are the ghost hitchhikers. One example of this kind of occurrence is the girl who tries to get cars to stop for her—and when they do, she vanishes. Another is the girl who runs across the highway in front of cars. Just when the car is about to hit her, she vanishes as well.

—Susan Miller
www.truckersue.com

GHOST RIDER ON HIGHWAY 666

I t was a warm summer evening in 2002 when I was pulling a load out of Gallup, New Mexico, to Florence, Arizona, on Highway 666. If memory serves me right, it was around three in the morning, a nice night to drive.

When I got down around the Four Corners area, I got the feeling I wasn't alone in my truck. It felt like someone was in the rider's seat. My truck became cold instantly, like the a/c kicked on high—but I didn't even have the a/c on. This all lasted maybe a minute.

When I got down to the truck stop, I was talking to some fellow drivers. I said, "have you ever come over the hill and hit a cold spot?" A couple guys said sometimes.

I mentioned it to the owner of place. He said sometime back when this road was first being used by truckers, a driver went off the side of the ridge and they never found him. So people say he rides with you to make sure you get past that spot of the road, so you don't meet the same fate as him.

I've traveled that route since and have had the same feeling more than once. In 2003, they renamed the highway U.S. 393, but old highway signs still hang below the new ones.

Carl Smith—American Trucker

THE WITCH OF SOCORRO, NEW MEXICO

Well, it was 1994, and I was living in Albuquerque, New Mexico, with my now ex-wife, and our four children. And she had a grandmother who lived in Socorro, New Mexico, who was ill with lung cancer and was pretty much on her last days. And we needed to take a trip there to say our good-byes. We took her sister and my brother-in-law with us with our children in my van and headed over to Socorro.

On the way into town, we ended up dropping by her sister's house. And we came down her street to this one church that was very beautiful. I don't remember the name, but it's just very beautiful. I just remember a very peaceful feeling once we came over there. Once we stopped by my sister-in-law's house, we brought her to her grandmother's house. And it, you know, it was a very somber but pleasant visit. Sad.

We decided to drive into town to get something to eat, with my wife, my sister-in-law and my brother-in-law, and the kids. And we were driving down the road, and one of them suggested that we should go look for this house that was owned by a woman named Sybil North,* who was supposed to be the town witch.

And I didn't have a very good feeling about it, but I was

outnumbered three to one. It was quite nerve-racking at first, because, you know, I've had my experiences in the past, so . . . So anyway, we went to get something to eat, and it's getting late. And it's getting quite dark. I was hoping they forgot about it. So we ended up piling in the vehicle, and the kids were pretty tired, so they kind of knocked out quite quickly. And then they said, "Okay, let's go and see if we can find where she lives." And I still had a really bad feeling about it—and I was unfamiliar with the area.

So we ended up driving through the town; it's not a very big place, but, you know, I was unfamiliar. We were driving through the main roads. And the sister-in-law suggested that we drive down this one road that was quite long but very dark because it didn't have any streetlights at all. And so we continued down that road 'cause they thought that could be where she lived. They're telling their stories about the things that she used to do, supposedly, and how mean and evil everyone considered this person.

And as we were turning . . . you know, we got to pretty much the turn in the road, and we went down even farther. It was like maybe two blocks, with no streetlights at all. So as we continued down the road, we came to what was like a cul-de-sac, like a dead-ending to the road. And you can . . . you can see the streetlights from there, but no lights in *our* area.

I was getting quite nervous with this because it was unfamiliar territory. And everybody was still excited to try to find it, but I was really nervous and kind of scared about it. I suggested that we just go back and head back home. And as I was telling them this, we saw headlights coming down the road the same way we went. And . . . which was quite scary because, you know, there were no houses around there or anything. And we knew it was a dead end. And you know, so we just kind of sat there and watched to find out who this person was.

And as the car came closer and closer, it was my wife's sister, the one that we had visited earlier. We were quite shocked that she found us in this dark, dark area that you can't really see off the main road. She pulls up and we ask what she was doing there and how she found us. And she said to us that something told her, she had this feeling . . . that we were lost and we needed to be found. Which I thought quite odd!

So my sister-in-law asked, "Do you know where Sybil North's house is?"

And she said, "Oh yes, it's just up the way."

I found that strange because I wanted to just leave, and as soon as that happened, she pulled up and knew exactly where we needed to be.

So we ended up following her out, and we kind of took a strange turn and went up this hill. And up this hill it was still kind of dark because it's off the main area. As we get to the top of the hill, she came and pulled up alongside us and said, "Her house is down this way."

And as we said, "Okay," she took off quite quickly in the opposite direction. We were already there, so we ended up driving by this house. It was like maybe two blocks down the road, and we ended up at a very spooky-looking house, you know, like a typical unkempt yard. The paint and everything was just not taken care of. It was kind of clichéd, but it was quite disturbing because everyone else around took care of their yards and all that. But it just seemed *off*. I thought maybe it was an abandoned house, but we could see a light inside this house. So someone *was* staying there.

I was quite worried because of the feeling that I had been getting through the day and because of the odd behavior of her sister needing to find us and showing us exactly where we needed to go. And so we ended up passing the house, and we had to do a U-turn because it was a two-lane road, which meant we had to go back past the house again. I was ready to get out of there.

As we passed her house, I said, "Good, we found it; we saw it. Let's leave." As we got close to the main road, the headlights on my vehicle started flashing on and off. Just on and off. On and off.

It was very weird. I was a diesel mechanic by trade, so I knew about electrical stuff and vehicles, because I've done quite a bit of that. I pulled off to the side of the road to check the switch and check the wiring, just check everything to make sure that nothing came loose and there was a bad connection. And I couldn't find anything.

Everybody—my wife and the sister-in-law and the brother-in-law—was quite scared by this point because of the coincidence of the lights flashing as soon as we passed the house. And they just kept on going on and off, on and off. I didn't know what else to do. So we got to the main road, to where I could get more light, and everybody's flashing their lights to tell me *my lights* are flashing. And as we went down the road farther I got under some light, and I wanted to check things. I checked the lights just to make sure there was no connection problem, and I just could not find anything. And soon after, I got back into the vehicle and we decided to go off the road to try to find my sister-in-law's house again. But we started hearing a noise in one of the tires like we were dragging something. So I had my lights going on and off, and I have the wheel making a weird noise, like a *shoo, shoo, shoo, shoo* sound.

Now I'm getting really scared. I was like, "Okay, this is bizarre." And everybody's still telling me my lights are flashing, and we're trying to get off the main road. We turn down a road. I get out again just to make sure there was nothing in the tire. And I checked all four; there was nothing that I could find, nothing dragging, nothing caught in any of the tires. Lights still flashing on and off. So we decide that we're going to go to my wife's sister's house, maybe spend the night, and then, you know, I'll check it out in the morning. And as I'm driving down one of the side roads, we make a turn, and it's still . . . I mean it just seemed like the wheel was getting louder, and the lights just, you know, kept on and off.

And as we turn this corner, it was like my headlights were just kind of, like, "waking up." The lights flickered and then just came on real bright and stayed on. And the sound of the tire that I heard was gone. And I went on for maybe, you know, just a few more feet, and I stopped and I looked. I just wanted to see, did something fall out of the tire, or whatever? I turned the light switch on and off—everything seemed to be functioning properly.

As I started to get back in the van, I just stopped and looked to my left. We were actually in front of the church that I had seen earlier. And I was scared. And I was thankful.

I'm a firm believer that if you go looking for something bad, it will find you. You won't have to look very far. I'm not quite sure what it is, but I do believe that there's something. And I do believe that whatever it was *knew* that we were looking for it. I truly believe that the sister finding us, you know, down that dark road off the main road, where you couldn't even see us—and she knew how to find us—was quite coincidental. It wasn't like, "Oh, she saw us down there and we were lost." She said something *told her* to find us, that we were lost.

On the way home, all the way back to Albuquerque from Socorro, no one said a word. I checked everything out the next morning on the vehicle and I could not find one thing wrong. The car behaved for a few more years and then I got rid of it.

I truly believe this experience was a good-versus-evil type of an issue. So, never again. I'm staying out of Socorro, trust me.

—Floyd "Von Frankenstein" Mayner

*Some names have been changed to protect privacy.

PART 4

Time Slips

Civil War soldiers and veterans of wars fought long ago in foreign lands; steam engines, phantom ships, and vintage trucks, all long since gone from this earth—how can it be that each of these historical anomalies have been seen by drivers traveling on U.S. roadways? These hardworking men and women are thinking about everyday things—deadlines, schedules, stopping for fuel or a fresh cup of coffee—when their journey somehow takes a turn into the bizarre, colliding with an event, a moment, or even a person from the past. From a request for help from General Custer to the ghost of a World War II officer saving a young man's life, these stories show that not every fallen soldier's story ends on the battlefield—and, sometimes, heroism lives on.

SOLDIER GHOSTS IN TEXAS

My ex-husband was a truck driver. His run was mostly Toronto to California, hauling produce for years. I went with him on a few runs. We had many weird or freaky experiences, but one stands out as a good one.

We were in the truck one night sleeping somewhere in Texas when we heard someone around the truck. Cameron, my husband at the time, got up to go look around. He came back into the bunk shortly after, saying he had seen nothing out there but black night. We settled back into the bunk again, only to hear someone rap on the door. This time we both jumped up, wondering who in the hell would be out there in the middle of nowhere walking around. This time he got his gun and used the flashlight to see outside into the pitch darkness. There was no one to be seen. We had been robbed a few times in the past, so he got dressed and proceeded to get out and check the trailer and under the truck. I waited inside with doors locked. He yelled at to me to come out. He could hear something and wanted my opinion. I was reluctant, but went.

I walked with him to the back of the trailer. Off in the woods we could hear people talking in the distance, but couldn't make out what they were saying or how close they were—their voices seemed to move, from the woods we were parked by to the other side of the road in the other woods. We stood there for quite a few minutes listening. We were puzzled, but thought maybe it was someone's house close by in the woods having a party and we just could not see the lights of the house. So again we got back into the truck.

We decided to stay up and sit in the dark and just try to watch out into the night after letting our eyes adjust to the darkness. After what seemed like only a few minutes, we could see movement on the road ahead of us. It looked like a group of people crossing the road from one bush to another about a hundred feet in front of the truck. So my husband turns on the truck headlights, and we see nothing—it was like they disappeared.

Now we are getting scared because we both saw the same thing before we turned on the lights: a group of people walking across the road. We also heard them talking. We sat looking at each other puzzled. Now we were really scared. We decided to investigate this more since we wanted to be reassured we weren't seeing things. There had to be an explanation for what we saw. So we got out of the truck with flashlights and walked up the center of the road, which no cars or trucks had been on for hours. We got to the spot where we thought the people had crossed and looked for signs in the long grass as we walked up the road with flashlights. There seemed to be no signs of grass bent over or disturbed, not even a critter track. We stopped walking, and again we heard voices and people talking in the woods, but could not see any lights in the woods or any sign of housing or habitation.

My husband wanted to walk into the bush—his curiosity gets his better side; me, I wanted to go back to the truck and leave. Cameron started into the woods down through the ditch. I followed, not wanting to be left alone. We walked into the thick bush about two hundred yards and could still hear people but couldn't make it out. It did not sound like a party or campers; it sounded like chanting to me. I stopped and said, "I'm not going any farther; I want to go back to the truck." Cameron agreed. He appeared to be more scared now. We started heading back to the road.

When we got to the road, we could see the truck; it was a sign of comfort, of home. We walked slowly, shining our flashlights into the grass at the edges of the ditch on each side. My husband was right beside me, step for step, when he said, "Do you see that guy over there?" as he grasped my arm to stop me from walking farther. I looked to where he was shining his flashlight and I saw a man in a Cavalry uniform at the edge of the woods just ahead of us. He faded away as soon as I saw him. My husband said, "Did you see him?"

I said, "Yes I did!" as he pulled me to start walking again. We were now steps from the truck, and mutually, without a word, we made a run for it. We reached the truck driver's door and I have never climbed in so fast in my life. We locked the door and sat in the dark for a few minutes looking around. Again we saw a large group of people crossing the road in front of us. My husband started the truck and said, "We aren't staying here tonight."

We sat in the truck waiting for it to warm up a bit and kept watching out the windows. We dimmed the dashboard lights and watched. We saw more groups cross the road, all going the same way, but they are like shadows, not really solid-looking. The truck was warm, and my husband put it in gear and started to roll slowly down the road. Both of us were looking with eyes as big as saucers. We felt safer now that we were moving, but were scared of what we had just seen but could not explain.

We didn't speak for about an hour. We hit the main highway and soon came to an exit with a motel sign. I knew then how scared my ex-husband was when he hit his signal and pulled into the hotel—was his first stay at a hotel in years. We talked about it to each other before we went to sleep in our new cozy rented bed. In the morning, Cameron circled the truck before we left and came in to get me. He said, "Come take a look at this."

When I went out into the morning sunshine I could see plain as day what he was showing me—there were many handprints on the sides of the dusty trailer. Like, hundreds of them, way bigger than mine would be. They were not fresh; they had dust over them, but there were a lot of them. We had just had the truck and trailer washed at a stop eight hours earlier.

We had bunked down on that back road and had never stopped in between the two stops. If the handprints had been made at the hotel, we felt they would have been fresher looking with no dust on top of them. It was a paved lot we parked in at the hotel, but yet was a dirt road we stopped to sleep on just off the highway.

We made it to Nevada to pick up our load of cucumbers that trip and really never talked about it again. We even got another hotel on the way back, which was a big treat for me . . . but safer. I stayed home for a while after that trip.

I don't know if others have had the same experiences in that area or out on the road, but that is one of my experiences.

—Barbara Dexter

GHOST TRAIN IN WYOMING AND CUSTER'S REQUEST

If you need more stories, I have a lot more stuff that did happen to me on the road. I drove nights mostly, during the time I drove OTR, and also, as it has been explained to me, I attract spirits, it seems. I had wrecked trains chase me in Wyoming late at night on the UP tracks while I was on I-80. I know I saw Custer near the Little Big Horn—stuff like that you never forget.

I ran team in 1997–98 with my father. He ran the day shift; I ran nights. Well, one night I was running west across I-80 between Laramie and Rock Springs, Wyoming, and I noticed that the headlights on the locomotive that was beside me looked different—they were bigger and dimmer somehow. So I looked a little closer and I saw it was a steam engine. I looked closer and saw it was an early American-style train. I then was like, anyone else seeing this? Two other drivers were like yes, but I did not want to be the first to admit it. Then about forty-five seconds later the train vanished, as if it was never there.

The George Custer story is harder to explain what happened. I was near the Little Big Horn area and it was a rare occasion—I was running solo at the time for Florilli. My father was not in the truck yet—still out from heart surgery. Well, I was tired, and all of a sudden I heard a voice saying, "Can you help me?" and it came from *inside* the truck. Now, I am running 68 mph at the time. I looked over, and there in buckskins was Custer, plain as day. He said, "I need reinforcements" and disappeared.

—Harold E. Benton

WOMAN STANDING BY HER CAR

This happened to my aunt and me when I was about seven years old. I'm not sure what the exact date was, but I know it was the mid-to-late 1990s.

My aunt and I were driving back from the mall, which was located thirty minutes from the town where we lived. There is a four-lane highway there now, but at the time of this story there was only a two-lane road that we could ride on since the highway wasn't there yet.

We were driving back, and we were about halfway home when we saw a car pulled off to the side of the road. Since my auntie didn't really see a lot of cars driving on the road, and the sun was beginning to set, she decided to pull over and see if this person needed help. My aunt was seventeen or eighteen years old at the time and she wasn't really the type of person to really do this type of thing, but she pulled over. We both noticed that there was an elderly woman standing by the car.

We stopped the car a few car spaces ahead of the woman's car. My aunt got out and said she would be right back. Since I was a little kid, I really didn't have much interest in sitting around waiting, so I vaguely remember sitting up and watching my aunt walk over to the woman. I remember being confused when my aunt stopped in her tracks and turned around. She seemed kind of irritated as she walked back, and she opened the driver's door again and sat down. She looked at me and was like, "I could have sworn there was an old woman and a car out there—you saw it, right?"

I remember staring at her, not really knowing why she was asking this. I had just watched her start walking back to the woman and saw her turn around while the woman was still there by her car. I meekly nodded my head and we both turned our heads to the back of the car and, sure enough, the car was there. My aunt sighed heavily and said something along the lines of, "It wasn't there a minute ago." She kept staring and said something about how maybe the woman was driving away before she got out of the car, but there was no way the woman could have driven away and back in the matter of seconds.

There were no side roads except maybe a half mile down the road. My aunt told me to come with her this time. We both got out of the car, and before I took more than a few steps the car and the old lady had disappeared. We both looked around in disbelief, and my aunt groaned in annoyance. She walked back to our car and said, "She can help herself now." I remember looking back as I pulled open the passenger door and there was still no car there.

As we sat down and started the car, I heard a loud screech. I looked around frantically and, sure enough, my aunt heard it, too, because she was doing the same thing. She looked into the rearview mirror and swore in a scared tone of voice as she put the car into drive. She seemed panicky and almost shaky as we drove off. I turned around to look out the back window and the car and the old woman were there. The old woman seemed as though she was running at us, but by this point we were already a distance down the road.

To this day, my aunt and I aren't sure what happened and whether or not the woman was real or just a product of our imagination. It felt real, though—and we both saw her. When we tell people this story, most people either just laugh it off or say we're lying. Some believe us. All I know is that the car disappeared whenever one or both of us got out of the car, but I don't know where it would go in a time span of seconds—especially since the woman appeared to be in her eighties or nineties. I have wondered if maybe the old woman was just a moment in time replaying itself that my aunt and I just happened to witness, but then why would she scream and chase us?

—The Miss

BLUE '55 CHEVY

In the summer of 1975, I was fourteen years old. Eight of us were bored on a hot summer evening, so someone suggested we have a séance. One of my friends missed his brother, who was killed in Vietnam in 1970, so the leader of the séance called to the spirit of Steve (the deceased). He then asked for a sign of Steve's spirit being present, then asked, if so, for the house's lights to go off—which, right then, they did.

I thought this was just a trick, so, as a sign, I asked for a 1955 Chevy to drive by the front of the house. No sooner were the words out of my mouth than we heard screeching rubber. We broke the circle and looked out the front window to see a 1955 blue Chevy speeding by, with no driver visible. We ran out the front door, jumped on our ten-speed bikes, and followed the taillights. We were happy to see the Chevy make a left turn, knowing the road was a dead end. When we arrived at the dead end shortly after, we found no car there. We even knocked on doors asking about it, and no one had seen or heard a thing. Never saw that car again . . . Strange, 'cause it was our neighborhood and the city we lived in was small (only twelve thousand people) at the time, so if that "car" would have been around, we would have seen it again. CREEPED me out.

—Brian J. Nolan

GHOST SHIP IN THE FOG

This happened when my two sisters and I were on a road trip to the West Coast. We had many strange experiences on this trip. We were traveling through Washington State along the Columbia Gorge to visit our cousin in Idaho. From Seattle, we went down the coast to Astoria, Oregon. After we left Astoria, it was evening, and we were looking for a hotel. The sun was setting, but we could still see the sun on the ocean.

All of a sudden, this huge fogbank rolled in. We saw a small sailboat in front of the fogbank, and we thought, well, they're kind of running along in front of the fog. You could see the front of the boat through the fog at times, and then the fog would get very thick and dark, and then it would get a little thinner. Suddenly, the fog started to get darker and darker. Even the atmosphere changed; it felt like there was an electric charge in the air. We were all looking at this strange fog, when, suddenly, a ship came out of it! It looked like the legendary *Flying Dutchman*. The ship had three masts—it was *huge*. It came out of the dark fog, ran along the front of it for just a few seconds, and then went right back into the fogbank. I grabbed my camera, hoping the ship would come out again. I did get a picture of the sun behind the fog just a few seconds after the ship had gone back into it, so at least I have that—but no *Flying Dutchman*.

I think the thick fog somehow allowed the ghost ship to manifest. Both my sisters and I saw it, and we couldn't believe what we were seeing.

—Cheryl Prenevost

STRANDED FAR FROM HOME

I was a seventeen-year-old student, broke and stranded at the Pan Am Halfway House, an old British officers' quarters at the airport in Karachi, Pakistan. It was December of 1965. I had been between planes, on my way from Istanbul, where I had been in an isolation ward with spinal meningitis, to Bombay to meet my ship, a "floating college campus." A war broke out in Kashmir, a contested province between Pakistan and India. All flights to India were canceled. I had been stuck at the old Pan Am barracks for almost two weeks. The makeshift hotel looked just like the British fort in the old Cary Grant movie *Gunga Din*.

The Pakistanis had torched the U.S. Embassy in Karachi and cut off all forms of international communications. I had no way of telling my family where I was, and no one to turn to for financial help.

The hotel manager asked me if I had any money to pay for my lodging and meals, and I told him I didn't have nearly enough. I had four JFK fifty-cent pieces, two packs of Marlboros, and a day to come up with a couple hundred dollars for room and board money. The manager said that I had one more night before he had to report me to the authorities, who would probably put me into a Pakistani debtors' prison.

I had found one book to read, a beat-up old paperback about the sinking of the German battleship *Graf Spee* in Montevideo Harbor in 1940, so I spent my "last afternoon" reading it.

That evening, I went to the bar, determined to get as sloshed as I could on my last two bucks. As I nursed my first cuba libre, I was amazed to hear a Brazilian samba. I turned to see a tall, tanned, aristocratic-looking gentleman in a white tropical suit enter the bar. He was carrying a portable tape recorder. He looked like a character right out of *Casablanca*. He took the stool next to me. We were the only people in the place.

I asked him, in Spanish, where he was from. He told me he was from Montevideo, Uruguay. In the course of the conversation, he told me that his name was Victor Hague and that he was working as an engineer for General Electric on a dam project in Kashmir, and that he was headed home until the war blew over. I told him who I was and that it was quite likely I would be hanging around Pakistan, probably behind bars, for a while. He asked me to join him for dinner. I gladly accepted.

We went into the dining room, the same Victorian British officers' mess that you saw in *Wee Willy Winkie,* and, over the oxtail soup and lamb curry, we talked. I told him that I had been reading a book about the *Graf Spee* and Montevideo, Uruguay. He commented that it certainly was a coincidence, because he had actually witnessed the sinking of the battleship. He talked for quite a while about how the ship, badly damaged in battle, had been scuttled in deep water just outside Montevideo Harbor. He recalled that the captain had wrapped himself in the old imperial German flag and committed suicide.

After dinner and brandy, Victor said he had a very early plane to catch and went to his room. I never saw him again.

I went back to my room to get one last good night's sleep before they came to take me away.

At 6:00 A.M., I awoke to a sharp knock on the door. I opened the door, and, instead of the constable, it was the hotel manager. He said that I should dress immediately and get my things packed, and then came the bombshell: the manager said that the gentleman that I'd had dinner with had paid my hotel bill and left me a ticket for Pan Am Flight 2 to San Francisco, which was leaving in forty-five minutes.

Victor Hague had, in all probability, saved my life.

After I got back to the States, I contacted General Electric in an effort to locate Victor Hague, but they had no record of anyone by that name on their payroll.

Almost five years later, I was in Buenos Aires, and I took a boat across the Mar del Plata to Montevideo to see if I could find Victor and his family. I talked to the commissioner of police, and he personally helped me search through the hall of records, but we found no listing of a Victor Hague anywhere in Montevideo or its suburbs.

A few years ago, I ran across some obscure German naval records. There was a junior officer named Victor Hague on the crew of the *Graf Spee*. He was killed in battle and buried at sea in 1940.

—Joel Whitehurst

INCIDENT AT LOST RIVER

I was hauling a load of lumber through eastern West Virginia, out of Virginia, when I experienced something that I can only describe as a *Twilight Zone* event. There are no ghosts in this story, but that only adds to the eeriness of it.

I have been a trucker for many years, and have put many miles behind me over the years. I picked up a load of lumber in northern Virginia and was traveling Route 55, a two-lane road through West Virginia, on my way home for the weekend. Route 55 goes through Petersburg, Moorefield, and Seneca Rocks, West Virginia. I remember crossing a covered steel bridge over the Lost River. I knew that I would be in Baker in just a short time. I had planned on stopping in Baker for a soft drink and a short break. I was pretty tired, and that is probably why I was side tracked.

I don't remember making any turnoffs or exits from Route 55. Once I reached Seneca Rocks, I was going to head west on 33 toward Elkins, and from there it was only an hour and a half to home.

After I crossed the bridge, I noticed that I had been driving for an awful long time. The trip from Baker to Moorefield is only about thirty minutes. When I looked at my watch, I had been driving about three hours longer than it should have taken me. As I was driving along, I noticed that I was on a strange road, not Route 55 that I had driven time and time again.

I was having to pull hills that weren't there before and use the low side of the transmission. It was taking me an excessive amount of time to drive this strange road—up one side and down the other. Out of one curve, only to go into another. I got so mad, I started beating myself up. I couldn't believe that I allowed myself to get so tired driving that I would take a wrong turn and end up lost on a wrong road. I quickly grabbed my road map, and in only a few minutes found that I must have been heading back to Virginia via a different route, 258, I think. This was really going to put me behind schedule, and I was furious with myself. How stupid I was.

I looked at the map and tried to find an alternate route back to Moorefield. The only roads on the map were dirt roads through the hills. There was no way I was going to try to drive a sixty-foot tractor-trailer through the woods. The only way to get back on track was to go on to Virginia and pick up Route 28 back to Seneca Rocks or find a place to turn around and back track to where I made the wrong turn. This is where I realized that something was wrong.

As I drove along, I noticed that the road was unusually smooth, no potholes, no rough places at all. I looked for a wide place or a driveway, or someplace big enough to turn around. There wasn't a wide place or driveway anywhere. There were no guide rails, though this road was hilly and curvy. It was so curvy that my trailer was crossing way over the center of the road in every curve, and I was having to drive across the center of the road so my trailer didn't go off the road on the other side. This is when I noticed that there were no yellow painted center lines or white painted edge lines. Where in the world was I?

The longer I drove, the weirder it got. There were no road signs, no mailboxes, no utility poles, no wildlife, and, worst of all, for three hours of driving, I never met or saw one single other vehicle. I grabbed my map again and tried to determine where I was. As I looked at my map, I noticed that I would be coming to a small town called Mathias, and then, just a few short miles more, I would go through another small town called Lost River. I finally saw a sign that read Mathias. I was relieved; I was no longer lost, for I was at least on the road to Route 28, even though I would be late. As I entered Mathias, I expected to see houses, cars, and maybe some people, a post office, and a store or two. There was nothing. No driveways, homes, stores, people, cars, painted lines, road signs, mailboxes, nothing. I thought it was pretty strange, but a lot of places in West Virginia have just a sign designating a town, and a few miles later there would be all these things.

The next thing I saw was a sign that read Lost River. I pondered for a moment and wondered what happened to Mathias. As I continued to drive along, Lost River didn't have any homes, mailboxes, or anything, nothing, just this incredibly smooth paved road with no painted lines or guide rails. I grabbed my map again and was relieved that in about thirty minutes or so, I would finally make it to the intersection of Route 28. I had been driving on this road for at least three hours, and I was really getting tired.

About the time I expected to reach 28, I looked up ahead, and

I finally reached a town with cars, people, homes, utility poles, and, yes, even painted lines on the road. To my amazement, I was in Moorefield. I was flabbergasted. Why did it take me over six hours to drive a three-hour trip through this stretch of road? Before anyone thinks I went to sleep and miraculously made this drive half-conscious, when I checked the mileage on the odometer, I had driven 70 miles and three hours out of my way, and when I entered Moorefield, I was on Route 55.

I had never left Route 55; I never made a wrong turn, but I was definitely on a road in the twilight zone, and I shudder to think what might have happened if I had stopped anywhere on this road and gotten out of the truck. If I had stopped, it would have had to be in the middle of the road, because there wasn't even a wide enough place on this road to pull off.

An old trucker friend of mine had a weird look on his face when I told him about this strange drive. He looked like he saw a ghost. He told me that when he was driving truck years ago, he had heard stories that were similar to mine that happened along this same stretch of road, but he didn't personally know any of these other drivers, so he dismissed it as an old trucker story. My friend told me that there is something weird about that area of West Virginia. He told me about his experience:

He was driving his pickup truck on Route 28 toward Seneca Rocks. He knew he would be at Seneca Rocks in about fifteen minutes from where he was. He had driven this area time and time again and had spent a large part of his life in Romney at a school for the deaf, so he was very familiar with the area. He said that in the time that you snap your fingers, he was from where he was to Seneca Rocks. It happened so fast that he slammed on his brakes and slid out of the road and almost crashed.

Shaken up, he got out of his pickup and walked over to the little store there to calm down and get a soft drink. This is when he looked at the clock on the wall and looked at his watch, and he had gotten to Seneca Rocks fifteen minutes early, for his watch was fifteen minutes slower than the clock on the wall.

In July a couple years after my strange experience, I took my wife to visit her family in Virginia. On the way back home, I told my family I was going to take them through the twilight zone. I just had to go back to this place to see where I was. As we went through the steel bridge, I described that this is the last thing I remembered seeing until I reached Moorefield. When we got to Baker, I made a left turn on 258 and told my family that I don't remember making this turn in the truck, but I must have. In about twenty minutes, we got to Mathias, and, to my surprise, there were houses everywhere, cars, people, and 258 had painted lines all the way. I want to note that when I was in the truck, the road was smooth, but it was not freshly paved. About nine miles more, we made it to Lost River, and there were stores, a post office, homes, people, cars—I couldn't believe it. I said, "I swear, these things weren't here before."

I don't remember the name of the state park on down the road from Lost River, but I told my family that we would drive that road to Moorefield; it goes through the woods, and it must have been the road I was on.

When we got to the park, there is a gigantic sign that reads "no trucks." I knew that if I had seen that sign I would not have continued on it in a truck. We drove several miles on this road, and it seemed eerily familiar, but there were wide places, mailboxes, and scattered homes. I told my family that I had to have been on this road in the truck, but I didn't know how. After we crested the last hill, I realized that there is no way I could have driven my truck on this road. About halfway down this hill, there is a switchback, and there is no way I could have pulled my trailer around it. No way. It would have taken dozers and wreckers to slide the trailer around this curve, and it probably would have done extreme damage to the truck, and trailer, so I determined that this is not the road I drove. When we reached the end of this road, it intersected with another road that leads into Moorefield from a different direction; then I knew that I did not drive my truck on that road through the woods. To this day I do not know where I was.

—Laken L. Eubank, Jr.

THE UNSEEN WAR

This story takes place when I was about twelve years old. I was traveling with my dad up to a remote place in Montana called Cut Bank. From what I can remember, it was only fifteen minutes from the Canadian border, but for me being a young military-history fanatic, all I could think about was the battle in which General Custer and his 7th Cavalry were slaughtered by their enemies. This may be why, on a very cold night in a remote part of Montana, I was awakened by the sound of yelling and screaming. Thinking it might be some kids playing a prank or worse, I grabbed my pocketknife and flicked it open. I opened the drapes of the sleeper. Under a moonlit and star-filled Montana night, I looked at the landscape ahead, and I swear I could see army soldiers being slaughtered by Indians. What happened next horrified me beyond comprehension.

As I looked out the window, the Indians looked at me. This seemed to provoke the ghosts of these war-painted warriors to make their way to the truck. My heart caught in my throat as the Indians began unloading arrows at the truck—but somehow, 7th Cavalry soldiers appeared beside the truck. They cut down the Indians and rode off. As they did, one of the soldiers saluted and nodded to me. I crawled back into the sleeper, shaking violently. My dad was sound asleep. When we continued on our trip the next day, he looked at me in the passenger seat. I was still visibly shaken. Thinking I was joking around, he said, "You look like you've seen a ghost."

I muttered "No shit," but didn't tell him about my experience. What made it seem so real was that on the passenger side of the truck were bloodstains. My heart jumped as I closed my eyes. When I opened them, the bloodstains were gone. I wondered what had caused them. But as I wondered, I also began to fear going back to sleep.

The next day we arrived in Cut Bank and unloaded our cargo, then proceeded back toward Utah. I was glad to leave Montana. But that night, a phantom soldier from the 7th Cavalry paid me a visit. What he said to me was almost like a vision of the future: "You will do the 7th Cavalry proud, son." Then he simply vanished. I woke up in a cold sweat and looked at my watch. We were finally in Utah.

Was this solider trying to send me a message? What the solider said to me seemed to come true in 2009, when I found, and safely returned, a 7th Cavalry patch.

—Darrayl Hayward

THE ARROW POINTS NORTH

This is a story based on an experience I had during the Arrow Trucking shutdown. It was a chilly December night in 2009. I was patrolling the yard; there were seven trucks in the yard that night. I was alone, and all of a sudden I felt a chill in the air. I looked to a Kenworth that had the POW/MIA insignia on it. I saw a man in his early thirties walk toward the truck. I pulled my baton from its holder and extended it, ordering the man to step away from the truck. He turned to me as if he understood me and looked down at the step of the truck. I motioned the baton in a "back away" kind of way. Suddenly, the man walked away and seemed to vanish into thin air. What struck me is this man wore a military uniform similar to the one my father wore back in Vietnam. I walked to the truck; my hand holding the baton was shaking. I looked down at the step and there were two patches, a POW/MIA patch and the patch belonging to the famous 7th Cavalry. I picked them up.

I looked at the patches and felt them; sure enough, they were real. I knew these belonged to a former Arrow driver, but what struck me is the man that appeared to me was wearing a military dress uniform similar to the one seen in the movie *We Were Sol-*

diers. He appeared to be sad; his eyes were empty. He had taken the 7th Cavalry patch off his uniform and placed it on the step of the truck. I spent the next few weeks tracking down the owner of these patches, and they were eventually returned to the driver.

—Darrayl Hayward

THE TRUCK IN THE MONFORT LANE

*T*o all my hardworking 'meat-hauling' friends, retired or at rest—I miss them all!

The Monfort lane—that was the affectionate nickname for the left lane on Interstate 80 in Colorado, named after the Monfort trucks than ran regularly on I–80 from Greeley, Colorado, to New York. The Monfort Company trucks were fast and were commonly seen in the left lane passing something. This is a story from one of their drivers.

The evening of June 18, 1974, was one of the worst, if not *the* worst, tornado outbreaks in Midwest history. Loren piloted his A-model Kenworth through Chicago on old 80 and crossed the Mississippi River into hell. Hail and rain hammered his truck as he passed Walcott, Iowa, headed west at about 8:00 P.M. He slowed down considerably. He wanted to stop, but he and his co-driver were given seventy-five hours to complete their New York turn, and if he could just get to Omaha, he could hand the truck over to his co-driver and make it back to Greeley on time.

By the time he got to Des Moines, the CB (which was still a new tool for truckers then) was blaring away reports to get off the road because it was too dangerous to drive. Then came the news that Ankeny, Iowa, was just destroyed by a tornado and there was no information on how many died. Loren weighed his odds and pushed on.

The weather had settled down considerably by the time he reached Stuart, Iowa, but the roads were still wet from the horrible storms that had just passed. He noticed there was no eastbound traffic, and he thought the CB reports must have convinced everyone to wait it out in Omaha. Putting the brownie into the big hole, he kicked his speed back up in normal Monfort fashion and began to relax. He was *too* relaxed, after being on an adrenaline rush for the better part of five hours fighting the weather. He began to doze. Nodding awake, he shook his head and slapped himself in the face to wake up a little. He noticed he was coming up on the Adair, Iowa, exit and there was still no eastbound traffic.

He checked his mirrors and noticed a truck gaining on him. It was maybe a mile behind him, its lights disappearing and reappearing as they went up and down the hills of western Iowa. Loren looked at his speedometer. He was running 70. What the hell has that truck got in it? he thought—it was obviously gaining on him. By the time Loren got to the bottom of the next hill, the truck overtook him and passed him. It sounded like a quiet jetliner—it had to be maybe a late 1950s or early 1960s B-model Mack with a box trailer hooked to it. It was all chromed out and looked like a metallic blue color, but it was too dark to know for sure. Loren noticed a small blue flame at the tip of both exhaust stacks as it whooshed by him in the Monfort lane.

Looks like we will get to the big O real quick, he thought,

as he floored the throttle in an attempt to keep up. His 350 Cummins just didn't have it. Knowing full well what an Endt 673 Mack engine was capable of, Loren couldn't understand how the truck had been able to pass him. As he watched that beautiful rig pull away from him and crest the next hill about three quarters of a mile ahead of him, Loren was wide awake, thrilled about what he had just seen that little Mack do.

As the Mack began to disappear over the hill, Loren saw the brake lights come on. Loren thought, okay, what's up? He decelerated fast, figuring the driver of the Mack must have seen something like a state car or debris on the road from the storm. Loren crested the hill and saw nothing but complete darkness—then he saw something at the edge of his lights that horrified him. He hit the binders hard and squealed to a stop. There was a livestock truck on its side blocking both westbound lanes. It had a full load of hogs as he saw maybe fifty of them dead on the road. They looked like human bodies in his headlights, and it had scared him. He had to think quick as he was worried about traffic coming from behind him, so he turned on his four-ways and put the truck almost sideways in the road. Not even thinking about waking his co-driver, he lit two of the four fuses he had. Just then a car crested the hill from the east. He frantically waved the fuses to get them to stop. They did, just in time.

It was a station wagon with a mom, dad, and three sleeping kids on their way to Colorado on vacation from Indiana. The mom jumped out of the car after seeing that there had been a wreck. She told Loren she was a nurse and asked if she could help. Loren replied, "The driver, I can't find the driver!"

She ran into the dark where the demolished cab lay. She came back a couple minutes later with her hands over her mouth; Loren knew the driver was dead. At that very moment, a very welcome sight appeared from the west—one of those big Chrysler Iowa State patrol cruisers with its light bar lit up. The officer was using his spotlight to find the wreck. As help started to arrive, the first officer on scene talked to Loren about what he had seen. He thanked him for stopping traffic, as someone would surely have run into the wreckage. Loren replied, "I would have hit it if it wasn't for the truck ahead of me hitting his brakes like he did."

The officer said, "The truck ahead of you?"

Loren replied, "Yeah, a blue Mack was hauling ass westbound. Passed me like I was standing still. I saw his brake lights as he crested that hill back there."

"Son," the officer said, "I ain't seen nothing coming from the east in over two hours."

A cold chill hit Loren. He said, "Well, where in the hell is he then?"

The officer went back to his cruiser and scanned the area with his spotlight, fearing the truck Loren described went across country and wrecked. Nothing. As the livestock wreck was moved, Loren thought about what he had seen and the Mack that possibly saved his life. He began to remember details like the blue flame from the pipes and the trailer. It was an old icebox trailer. He thought it seemed awfully short! Hell, they haven't used those in fifteen years! Where did he go? he thought to himself. Another chill ran up his spine as he began to wonder if the truck existed at all. There was no way he could have gotten himself past the wreck without hitting it. He was going way too fast.

Loren walked back to the vacationing family and asked them if a truck had passed them before they stopped. They said, "You're the first truck we have seen in hours." Then the mom looked up at him from the station wagon and said, "Thank you for saving our lives." Loren looked into the car. In the backseat of the station wagon were three beautiful little kids. One was just a baby, sleeping comfortably, totally unaware of what was going on outside the car. Loren said with a lump in his throat, "I can assure you, ma'am, I had nothing to do with it."

—Gary M. Vaughn
www.garyvaughnasanauthor.com

THE WALL

It was April 8, 1979, almost four years to the day the last U.S. military helicopter left the roof of the embassy in Saigon— leaving the country and its spoils to the victorious General Nguyen Van Toan of the North Vietnamese Army. It wasn't a day I wanted to remember. I hadn't even thought about that day for years—not since I watched our defeated troops' withdrawal on television. I returned home from Vietnam in 1970, and at that time I was still naive enough to believe we were actually winning over there. However, today was different—today I met someone that reminded me of the significance of that day—of the war— and of the friends I had not seen in years.

I stopped at the all-night diner in Newburgh, New York. Their food was always a little too garlicky, but it was tolerable; their coffee on the other hand was always strong enough to strip paint— just the way I like it. I was on my way to a small town called Red Hook for a 10:00 A.M. appointment with a crane; it was about a two-and-a-half-hour drive from Newburgh, so I was not in any particular rush. I was, however, looking forward to a good night's sleep and a full stomach. There were half a dozen trucks in the parking lot with their engines idling, but there was only one other driver in the diner. Within a few minutes after my arrival, he dropped a couple of dollars on the counter and left, leaving me the sole diner.

As I pushed my plate away, I noticed movement in my peripheral vision from the far end of the restaurant. Thinking I was alone, I turned toward the movement. In the last booth, there was a young marine sitting quietly with his hands folded on the table. I wondered to myself how I hadn't noticed him before. I was prepared to leave, but something compelled me to sit and talk with him for a while. I caught the waitress's attention, indicating I wanted two cups of coffee brought to the booth in the corner. I asked the marine if he minded if I joined him for a few minutes. "No sir—please—sit down," he responded. There is nothing like a marine to be sickeningly polite—and make you feel like an old man at the same time. As I slid into the booth across from him, I noticed the four rows of combat ribbons on his chest, and his rank. He was a lance corporal. He couldn't be much more than twenty, or twenty-one years old. He would have been maybe fourteen when these medals were handed out. I recognized them, because I have most of the same ones. He wore the yellow, red, and green Vietnam Service Ribbon, right next to the green and white Vietnam Campaign Ribbon. One row up, dead center, he wore the uniquely distinctive red, green, and yellow Vietnam Unit Citation Ribbon. In the top row, he wore, among others, the Purple Heart with an oak leaf cluster—meaning he had been wounded more than once. I was fascinated by the Unit Citation Ribbon. I pointed to it, and asked him to tell me about it.

"This one?" he asked, as he pointed to the Unit Citation on his chest.

"Yes," I said.

"It is for the battle at Khe Sanh," he answered. "Have you ever heard of it?"

"Oh yes, I have," I told him. "I was at the battle of Hue." His eyes widened at the name, then became distant as he remembered the war and the memories. The waitress brought us our coffee and set the bill in front of me. Once she was out of earshot, he began to tell me *his* story. It was a story I knew quite well. I had friends that were part of the Third Marine Division that were under siege for seventy-seven days. Most of them died at Khe Sanh defending an abandoned airbase.

Over the next hour he convinced me that he was in fact the real deal, that he had been there and suffered all of the indignities the rest of us suffered while we were over there. He talked of friends he had lost, and how much the experience had changed his outlook on life. While we talked, I noticed a few drivers coming and going, most stopped only long enough to get their thermos filled or eat a slice of pie. No one paid any particular attention to us, and this young marine seemed oblivious to everyone—except me, that is. At the counter, an elderly driver sat down and ordered a cup of coffee. This was the first time the marine paid the slightest attention to anyone else in the diner. He watched the old man intently; he wasn't at all surprised when the driver started coughing uncontrollably. I listened as the old driver choked and coughed, watching the expression on the marine's face the whole while. He was concerned; I could see it in his eyes. Finally, the old man's coughing fit subsided; he paid his bill and left.

I looked at my watch and realized I had been talking to this young man for almost three hours, and I didn't even know his name. I introduced myself, and he told me his name was Timothy—Timothy O'Hara. I took a napkin and wrote out my name and number. I left it in front of him and told him he could call me anytime—for any reason—even if all he needed was to talk. He turned his head and watched as the old man that had been coughing at the counter only moments before turned out of the parking lot heading north. I looked up just in time to see the words "Sea Bright" in bold black letters across the back doors of the trailer. I picked up the check and turned toward the cashier, when he said very softly, "Not yet sir; don't leave yet." I turned and asked him to repeat what he had just said; I apologized for being a little hard of hearing. "Please don't go yet sir; just stay a few more minutes," he said. I sat down again. I asked if he needed a ride somewhere, and said I would be more than happy to drop him anywhere he wanted to go. He smiled and thanked me, but explained that he was waiting for someone. He had made a promise to a friend years before to meet right here at this diner on the anniversary of their rescue from Khe Sanh. We sat in silence for almost ten minutes when he finally said that I could go now, that it was safe.

In the truck, I tore a page from my notebook and wrote down the name Timothy O'Hara. I folded it and put it in my wallet. I wouldn't look at it again until five years later.

It was getting late, and my opportunity to get a good night's sleep was rapidly diminishing. I pulled out of the parking lot and headed north to Red Hook. The river road going north to Albany is a beautiful drive during the day, and it is fast and traffic-free late at night. I loved to drive it. I was back up to cruising speed after passing through Poughkeepsie, and, as I rounded a blind curve, I slammed on the brakes, for just in front of me two semis had just slammed into each other. The trailers hadn't even stopped rocking as I rounded the curve. The truck that apparently caused the accident was heading north when he crossed into the southbound lanes, hitting the other truck head-on, causing a chain reaction. The force of the impact had popped open the trailer doors of the northbound truck. As they swung freely, I managed to read the words "Sea Bright" in bold black letters. I pulled my truck to the shoulder and turned on my four-ways. I took a handful of road flares out of my side compartment, struck them, and threw them as far back up the road as possible. I went to the old man's cab, but the door was crushed shut from the impact. The driver's door window was shattered, so I climbed up and leaned in. The driver was dead; he had no pulse, but he did have white froth around his mouth and chin—I found out later he had apparently suffered a massive heart attack.

There were four trucks and five cars involved in the accident that night. There were three fatalities not including the old driver that suffered the heart attack. Had I left the diner when I tried the first time, I would have been running directly behind the old man when he had his heart attack. I would have been the fifth truck—and possibly the fourth fatality. I promised myself to one day locate Timothy O'Hara through the Marine Corps directory and thank him.

Washington, D.C., is one of the two worst cities in America to drive a truck in. The other is Salt Lake City. They are both designed like a set of enormous traffic circles radiating out from one central location. Each quadrant is numbered and lettered exactly the same except for the directional indicators—like N.NW or S.SE. The compass points are calculated from either the Mormon Temple or the Capitol Building depending upon which city you happen to be lost in at the time. I was in Washington, D.C., along with six other trucks in the fall of 1984. I was involved in a large equipment move for a trade show. We were led downtown in a convoy with police escorts. It was nice. I think had they not provided the escorts, I would probably still be driving around lost, looking for a large round building that wasn't the Capitol. Once we were unloaded, we were again escorted to the staging area, where we would park until the show was over, and then we would reload and leave town.

The next morning during breakfast, a few of the drivers were discussing taking a trip to see the Vietnam Veterans Memorial. It sits just adjacent to the National Mall. It was less than a half mile, and we figured we could walk that distance faster than drive, so we left on foot as soon as we finished breakfast. I had a few names I wanted to look up—one was my friend Kevin; we had been together since boot camp, and he died in my arms in 1968 during an ambush in Vietnam's Death Valley. Once we got there, I stopped at the welcome center. I looked at the directory and found his name and where it was located. I walked to the panel marked 70 E, the last date listed is March 25, 1968. I found Kevin's name and started to rummage around in my pockets for a pencil and piece of paper so I could rub his name like everyone else was doing. I opened my wallet and found a long piece of notebook paper folded and stuffed into the corner. Unfolding it, I saw the name I had written on it five years before: Timothy O'Hara. I had completely forgotten Timothy and how he quite possibly saved my life that night in New York. I didn't want to destroy his name by rubbing Kevin's name over it. People were friendly enough, and I quickly found someone with a sheet of notebook paper they were willing to give me. I walked back to panel 70 E to rub Kevin's name when, all of a sudden, I was struck by something I really didn't expect to see. Two rows down and one name over—there it was—Timothy O'Hara. I found his name in the archives. Lance Corporal Timothy O'Hara died March 24, 1968, at Khe Sanh. As my own reflection stared back from the sea of black granite, with Timothy's name floating in the middle, I wondered if the person he was waiting for that night ever showed up—or would he be obligated to repeat the meeting ritual every anniversary until he does. Or, was Timothy possibly there that night for another reason?

—Terry L. Aldershof
www.anatomy-of-a-haunting.com

SHARE *YOUR* HAUNTED ROAD STORY.

Annie would like to hear your true ghost stories and haunted road experiences. If you would like to be part of the Trucker Ghost Story Project, please send your story or contact information to Annie Wilder at truckerghoststories@yahoo.com.

Copyright Acknowledgments

About the Editor

Raised in a family with Irish-German roots and strong intuitive abilities, stories of the unseen world of angels, ghosts, and lost souls have always been part of Annie Wilder's everyday life. She is the author of two previous books, *House of Spirits and Whispers,* a true account of living in a haunted house, and *Spirits Out of Time*, a collection of true family ghost stories. Annie has been a guest on the acclaimed *Coast to Coast AM* radio program, and her house has been featured in several print news stories and television programs, including the Biography Channel show *My Ghost Story*. Annie's home has been investigated by teams of ghost hunters and visited by a number of prominent psychics, including Linda Drake and Echo Bodine. Visit Annie online at www.anniewilder.com.